MEMORY MAKERS

PUNCH YOUR ART OUT 3

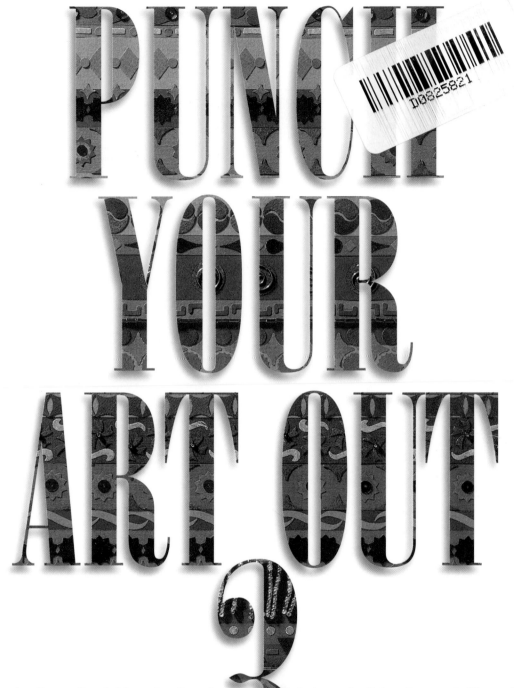

Creative Paper Punch Ideas for Scrapbooks With Techniques in Color, Pattern & Dimension

M
MEMORY
MAKERS
BOOKS

BOOK DIRECTORS	*Michele & Ron Gerbrandt*
EDITORIAL DIRECTOR	*MaryJo Regier*
ART DIRECTOR	*Sylvie Abecassis*
CRAFT DIRECTOR	*Pam Klassen*
IDEA EDITOR	*Pennie Stutzman*
ASSOCIATE EDITOR	*Kimberly Ball*
CONTRIBUTING WRITERS	*Kelly Angard, Lori Elkins Solomon*
STAFF ARTISTS	*Pamela Frye, Erikia Ghumm*
PHOTOGRAPHY	*Ken Trujillo, Brenda Martinez, Reid Portscheller*
SENIOR DESIGNER	*Susha Roberts*
DESIGNERS	*Karen Roehl, Pia Valeriana*
FEATURED ARTISTS	*See Artist Index on page 91*
FINISH ARTISTS	*Carmen Braaksma, Karen Gerbrandt, Ann Kitayama,*
	Pam Metzger, Chris Peterson, Michelle Pesce, Stacey Shigaya
LETTERING ARTISTS	*Michelle Pesce, Sande Womack*
EDITORIAL SUPPORT	*Dena Twinem*

MEMORY MAKERS® PUNCH YOUR ART OUT 3
Copyright © 2002 Memory Makers Books
All rights reserved.

Published by Memory Makers Books
12365 Huron Street, Suite 500, Denver, CO 80234
Phone 1-800-254-9124
First edition. Printed in the United States.

Library of Congress Cataloging-in-Publication Data

Memory makers punch your art out 3 : creative paper punch ideas for scrapbooks with techniques in color, pattern & dimension.
    p. cm.
  Includes bibliographical references and index.
  ISBN 1-892127-02-4
  1. Paper work. 2. Cut-out craft. 3. Scrapbooks. I.Title: Punch your art out 3. II. Memory makers.

  TT870 .M43 2002
  745.54--dc21

                                                                        2001059088

Distributed to trade and art markets by
F & W Publications, Inc.
4700 East Galbraith Road, Cincinnati, OH 45236
Phone 1-800-289-0963

ISBN 1-89212-702-4

Memory Makers Books is the home of *Memory Makers*, the scrapbook magazine dedicated to educating and inspiring scrapbookers. To subscribe, or for more information, call 1-800-366-6465. Visit us on the Internet at www.memorymakersmagazine.com

THIS BOOK BELONGS TO

_____

We dedicate this book to all of our Memory Makers
contributors whose innovative and incredible punch ideas
are the inspiration behind the art featured in these pages.

Contents

59

36

82

33

Mother's Day

AFTER TAKING OUR TRADITIONAL PHOTOS OF ME WITH EACH CHILD, I GOT TO ENJOY A RELAXING FAMILY GET TOGETHER WHERE THE MEN WORKED AND THE WOMEN WATCHED. NOW THAT'S A HOLIDAY!

Introduction

The world of punch art continues to amaze me. In the short time since we published *Memory Makers Punch Your Art Out 1* and *2*, literally hundreds of new punch designs have appeared. We are so fortunate that the punch manufacturers are accommodating our needs by providing us with the variety we desire. We can now work with squares, circles and spirals from mini to jumbo and every size in between. The countless new designs help fuel our creativity for new ideas, applications and innovative techniques.

In *Punch Your Art Out 3*, we have chosen to focus on two challenging areas of punch art—color and patterning. As you flip through the pages of this book, you will notice the chapters are broken down by color. We present the designs in this way to inspire and encourage you to experiment with traditional and eclectic color combinations.

Also, viewing the punch art in specific colors helps you to focus on the design. Every design in this book can be easily adapted to another color scheme for an entirely different look that works with your photos, theme or project. For instance, my Mother's Day page to the left has been adapted from a black-and-white design on page 73.

You may also notice that all the designs in this book are patterns and repeating images. Patterns give you a way to utilize your punches over and over again. We added a page in each chapter dedicated to showing how many different designs we could create with one single punch.

In addition to color and pattern, we thought it would be exciting to experiment with dimension and texture. There are so many fun and innovative accessories and papers available, and we wanted to play with them all—eyelets, wire, beads, vellum and more. I think you will love the drama and detail that these accessories bring to your punch art designs.

Similar to *Punch Your Art Out 1* and *2*, we worked with a lot of talented punch artists to bring you original and innovative ideas. I want to thank all of the artists for their fresh experimentation! I have truly been inspired. We are already anxious to get started on *Punch Your Art Out 4*.

"Every design in this book can be easily adapted to another color scheme for an entirely different look that works with your photos, theme or project!"

Michele

Practical Guide to Punches

Welcome to more of the fascinating world of paper punch art! All of the art featured in this book was created with craft punches—rugged little tools in which you insert a piece of paper and press down on the button on top, and out pops a punched shape or design.

Punches are available in hundreds of shapes, letters, numbers and more. Some punches allow you to create unique border designs and corner treatments; others offer an extended reach onto the paper you are punching. While punch names and sizes may differ slightly among manufacturers, one thing is certain: Punches continue to inspire us with their amazingly endless design possibilities.

On pages 92-95, you'll find a Punch Index that lists the majority of punches used to create the art showcased in these pages. For further convenience, here's just a small sampling of the various types of craft punches that you might find at local scrapbook or craft stores.

4 LARGE/JUMBO PUNCH
$1\frac{1}{16}$" to $1\frac{1}{2}$"*

6 SILHOUETTE PUNCH

7 FRAME/DOUBLE
FRAME PUNCHES

2 SMALL PUNCH
$\frac{5}{8}$" to $\frac{11}{16}$"*

3 MEDIUM PUNCH
$\frac{15}{16}$" to 1"*

10 DECORATIVE CORNER PUNCH

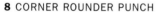

8 CORNER ROUNDER PUNCH

1 DOUBLE & MINI PUNCHES
$\frac{1}{16}$" to $\frac{5}{16}$"*

5 GIANT/SUPER/
JUMBO/MEGA PUNCH
$1\frac{1}{2}$" to 3"*

9 DECORATIVE CORNER
ROUNDER PUNCH

16 EXTENDED REACH PUNCH
$\frac{5}{16}$" to $\frac{3}{4}$"*; can reach up to 4"

13 CORNER LACE PUNCH

11 CORNER SLOT/
PHOTO MOUNTING PUNCH

18 HAND PUNCH

15 BORDER/EDGE PUNCH

17 SIX-IN-ONE PUNCH

14 DECORATIVE CORNER
LACE PUNCH

12 CORNER FRAME PUNCH

19 PUNCH KIT

1 DOUBLE & MINI PUNCHES

2 SMALL PUNCH

3 MEDIUM PUNCH

4 LARGE/JUMBO PUNCH

5 GIANT/SUPER/JUMBO/MEGA PUNCH

6 SILHOUETTE PUNCH

7 FRAME/DOUBLE FRAME PUNCHES

8 CORNER ROUNDER PUNCH

9 DECORATIVE CORNER ROUNDER PUNCH

10 DECORATIVE CORNER PUNCH

11 CORNER SLOT/PHOTO MOUNTING PUNCH

12 CORNER FRAME PUNCH

13 CORNER LACE PUNCH

14 DECORATIVE CORNER LACE PUNCH

15 BORDER/EDGE PUNCH

16 EXTENDED REACH PUNCH

17 SIX-IN-ONE PUNCH

18 HAND PUNCH

19 PUNCH KIT

Sizes, shapes and colors of punches are approximate and vary slightly among different manufacturers.

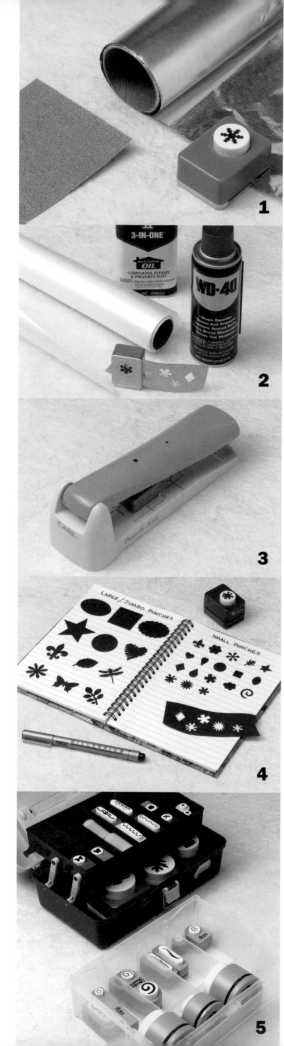

Punch Care & Troubleshooting Guide

Protect your investments and enjoy trouble-free punching with these handy tips.

1 SHARPENING PUNCHES

When punches become dull, try punching through heavy-duty aluminum foil to sharpen. If necessary, punch through a very fine grade of sandpaper, both right side up and upside down, to sharpen all edges.

2 STICKY PUNCHES

Punch through waxed paper to lubricate and "break in" new punches. If paper gets stuck in a well-used punch, place punch in freezer for 15-20 seconds. Metal will contract for easy paper removal. Once jammed paper is removed, lubricate the punch lightly with lightweight sewing machine oil or WD-40®. Clean excess oil away before using punch.

3 DIFFICULT PUNCH COMPRESSION

Make certain that the material you are punching through is not too thick. Use the palm of your hand and push down hard, or place the punch on the floor and gently step on it. There are also a variety of punch compression aids on the market to make punching easier.

4 PUNCH ORGANIZATION

Keep a small notebook handy that shows punched shapes from the punches you own, organized by size, type or theme of punch, to avoid duplicate purchases and for quick reference at your workspace. This will also help you quickly identify punch art designs or projects that you are equipped to make without having to dig through your punches.

5 PUNCH STORAGE

For years of service, store punches covered in a dry place to prevent rusting and dust. Many companies offer totes and storage containers made specifically for carrying and storing punches. Plastic bins—even large tackle boxes—work well for this purpose. Cleaned and dried empty film canisters make excellent storage compartments for small, leftover "punchies" or confetti.

Essential Tools & Supplies

In addition to craft punches, you will also need a few essential tools and supplies, most of which you probably already have on hand. These include:

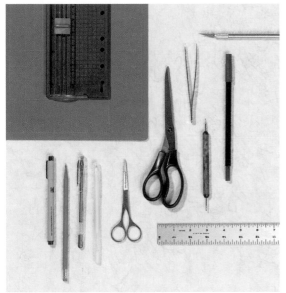

Acid- and lignin-free paper

Craft knife

Cutting mat

Metal straightedge ruler

Paper trimmer

Pencil

Photographs

Photo-safe adhesives

Pigment pens and markers

Self-adhesive foam spacers

Sharp scissors

Tweezers

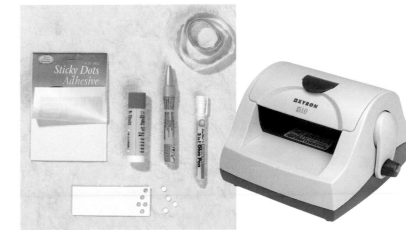

ADHESIVE APPLICATION

Photo splits or tapes can be cut to accommodate punched shapes. Pass paper through a Xyron™ adhesive application machine before punching for a quick, uniform application of adhesive. Glue pens are another great option.

OPTIONAL TOOLS

You'll also need the following tools to help you incorporate other craft supplies (see pages 14-15) to your punched designs for added texture and dimension:

Embossing stylus
Eyelet setter
Needle-nose pliers
Sewing or embroidery needle
Small hammer

Experimenting With Color

Color surrounds us everywhere. Speaking a universal language all its own, color is so abundant in our daily lives that it often goes unnoticed. But when faced with photos and a blank scrapbook page, color becomes quite personal—sometimes even intimidating.

If you weren't born with an intuitive eye for choosing great color combinations or your college thesis wasn't on color theory, then this simple color guide is just for you.

COLOR WHEEL

A color wheel is an inexpensive, centuries-old tool that can help you "dial up" fail-proof and striking color combinations. Available at art and craft stores, some wheels are very basic, including only primary (pure) colors—red, yellow and blue—which cannot be mixed from any other colors, and secondary colors—orange, green and violet—the combination of two primary colors.

Other wheels can be quite detailed, often subdivided to show a much larger color palette that includes tertiary colors, which are the result of mixing one primary and one secondary color. All color wheels come with user-friendly instructions. Select a fairly detailed color wheel; you will master it quickly but may outgrow a very basic color wheel more quickly.

What does all this mean for the scrapbooker or paper artist? Take a look at this two-sided color wheel. One side shows how to mix colors to create different hues—useful for mixing "that perfect hue" of paints or chalks for punched designs.

The dial on the other side is a "harmony" wheel. It illustrates color relationships or harmonies—valuable for selecting harmonious paper color combinations. On the following page, there are a number of examples of a color harmony wheel in use.

PAINT CHIPS

Paint chips, a simple alternative to the color wheel for determining harmonious color combinations, are available at most paint stores for free. One common type of paint chip sample shows one particular color and three to six descending shades, tints or tones of that color (below)—very useful for creating monochromatic (see example on next page) punch art designs. Another type of paint chip, although a little harder to find, are samples that show a number of different shades from different color families that harmonize well together (above). Punch a hole in the top of your paint chip samples and string them together on a metal ring to create a color selection "swatch book."

SELECTING PAPER COLORS

Before you begin, examine your photographs. List two to four major colors in the photos that best highlight the important aspects of the photos plus a neutral color, such as black, white or cream. Then select just one of the colors to be your "starting color." Spin the dial of a color harmony wheel and follow the directions on the wheel to see the possible color combinations. Or spread out some paint chips with your photos to help you find your "starting color" and to help determine other colors that would harmonize well.

Use your color wheel or paint chips and what you've learned here and on the next page, and you'll be selecting paper colors for your punch art with confidence!

Be sure to take your photos, color wheels and/or paint chips with you to the store when shopping for colored paper.

Fail-Proof Color Combinations

You don't have to be a color expert to achieve stunning punch art designs. These common color combinations prove that good use of color can be a great substitute for pattern, texture and dimension in your designs. *It's important to note that all of the punch art designs featured in this book can be re-created in any color combination to coordinate better with your photographs or page theme. Select colors in good light. Bright light or dim light will distort color perception.*

1 COMPLEMENTS

Complements are directly across from each other on the color wheel. They are equally powerful and, when used together in a design, make each other pop.

2 SPLIT COMPLEMENTS

Consists of choosing a color and using it with the colors on each side of its complement.

3 DOUBLE COMPLEMENTS

Pairs of complements that can be combined to produce a palette of four colors that look great together.

4 TRIADIC COMPLEMENTS

Think triangle. Uses three colors equally spaced from each other on the color wheel, such as the primary or secondary colors.

5 MONOCHROMATIC

Uses any number of shades, tints or tones of just one color.

6 ANALOGOUS

Because adjacent or neighboring colors are so similar they work well together.

7 ACHROMATIC

A colorless scheme that uses blacks, whites and grays.

8 INTENSITY

The dullness or brightness of a color is its "intensity." It's eye pleasing to mix similar intensities, such as using all pastels or all jewel tones.

9 BLACKS, WHITES, NEUTRALS

Black can deepen a color's value, thus "setting it off." White lightens or "softens" a color's value. Black and white look great with most other neutrals, including blacks, whites, browns and grays.

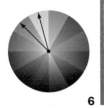

Adding Texture & Dimension

If you're like most punch art enthusiasts, once you've browsed the scrapbook aisles at your local craft store, beads, wires, paints, inks, and other colorful items beckon to you like sweets in a candy store. You may hesitate to purchase them. You may wonder if they are safe to use with photos or how to include these items in your scrapbook without adding extra bulk to the pages. A little creativity and care are all it takes to adapt these craft products to your needs, thus adding new texture and dimension to scrapbooks—and other paper crafts as well.

BAUBLES

Beads, buttons, rhinestones and sequins add a jewel-like quality to punch art. If the items are made of glass, stone or fired ceramic, they contain no acid and will not harm photos or scrapbooks. Plastic items are suitable as well—as long as they do not contain PVC. If you're not sure whether a bauble is photo-safe, encapsulate it or place it away from photos. Also, remember that baubles are hard objects that can potentially scratch your photos; don't place photos opposite these items on a facing page. To avoid adding excess bulk to a page, use small, flat objects whenever possible.

COLORANTS

The selection of colorants for scrapbookers has expanded beyond basic pens and markers to include chalk, paint, tinted glues, stamping inks and embossing powders—all widely available in acid-free versions made just for scrapbookers. Here are some hints for successful use of colorants:

♥ *Add chalk highlights to punched designs then spray the art with an acid-free fixative to prevent chalk particles from scattering.*

♥ *Although many paints and inks are acid-free and photo-safe, some—watercolors, for example—are not necessarily waterproof or fade-resistant. Protect painted and inked designs from light, moisture and accidental spills.*

♥ *Add sparkle without a mess with acid-free, photo-safe glitter glue or pearlescent glue.*

♥ *Dye-based stamping ink dries quickly and is good for general use. Pigment-based ink is more vibrant but takes longer to dry; it may be used alone or with embossing powder. Embossing ink is lightly tinted or colorless and is used with embossing powder. The powder protects inked images. Sprinkle it over damp ink and apply heat to transform your flat, inked image into an elegant, raised design.*

METALLICS

Metallic charms, wire, jewelry-making components, eyelets, embossing metal and fasteners add shine and luster to your page. Metallics do not pose a chemical risk to scrapbooks unless they contain iron, which rusts easily. Copper also has a tendency to corrode, but fortunately, many copper craft products are coated with protective sealant. Other noncorrosive metals may change colors over time and will add an antique feel to your layout.

Reserve metallics for special designs. Avoid heavy charms, opting instead for lightweight, flatter items. If possible, isolate metallics from photos so that they don't scratch the emulsions.

TEXTILES

Textiles add a finishing touch to punch art. Ribbon and embroidery floss "tie together" punched elements, weave borders, attach baubles and stitch designs, but they shouldn't touch photos. Plant-based fibers (such as cotton) contain lignin and may also contain damaging chemicals added during manufacturing. Both natural and synthetic textiles may contain fugitive dyes; test for color permanence by applying a moist cotton swab to the fabric to see if color spreads onto the swab. If a textile holds sentimental value, such as a ribbon from your wedding gown, it should be encapsulated to protect it from adhesive, light, dust and moisture.

ORGANICS

To lend a natural look to your punch art designs, try adding organic items such as pressed flowers and leaves, natural raffia—even tiny shells. These versatile items are great for page themes ranging from romance to the great outdoors. Adhering them to paper can be a challenge, however, because they are delicate yet bulky. Items holding sentimental value are best encapsulated, and others can be attached using double-sided tape or clear-drying adhesive. Plant-derived products such as pressed flowers, dried leaves and raffia contain lignin, so keep them away from photos.

Seashells are chemically stable, but their hard, sharp surfaces may scratch photo emulsions. Balance creativity with care, and you will produce punch art that is not only beautiful but long-lasting as well.

Tips & Techniques

These illustrated tips and techniques will help you achieve the most dazzling punch art designs possible.

Begin with a work surface that is clean and protected by a cutting mat. Make sure that your tools, including your punches, are clean, dry and sharp before you begin creating your punch art designs.

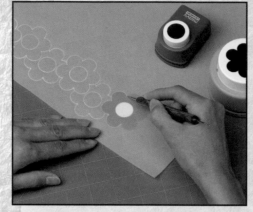

Embossing Punch out a shape from dark cardstock and place it underneath paper or vellum. Trace around the punched shape with an embossing stylus.

Interlocking Make interesting borders with just about any punched shape by simply interlocking the shapes before adhering to background.

Layering Create dimension by layering various sizes of the same punched shape using double-sided, self-adhesive foam spacers for desired height and lift.

Pen stroking Accent punched shapes with pen strokes. Simply use the pen of your choice to detail or outline the shape to make it stand out.

Punch guidelines Draw evenly spaced dots or "tick marks" for guidelines on back of paper for accuracy. Flip punch over; insert and align paper, placing marks where the center of punch should be.

Punch positioning Proper punch positioning ensures accuracy. Flip punch over to properly align over stamped design or over previous punch when repunching.

Removing guides To increase the versatility of a corner punch, use a flat screwdriver or a butter knife to remove the plastic guides as shown. Now you can use the corner punch to create a border.

Repunching Use paper that is larger than anticipated design. Punch smaller shape first. Flip punch over and repunch with a larger punch to create a new shape—thus working from the inside out.

Reverse imaging Reverse imaging creates a "positive/negative effect" achieved by layering two different colored punched shapes and slicing them together. Reassemble original shape, lining up the different colored pieces.

Shadowing Combining two monochromatic-colored punched strips of vellum, layered and mounted askew, gives the illusion of a cast shadow. See page 32 for another variation of shadowing.

Slicing & reassembly Slice or cut punched shapes and reassemble using different paper colors and patterns for a unique, multicolored effect.

Slicing in detail Bring realism to punch art designs by slicing in details for punched shapes that are organic in nature—such as leaves, flowers, trees and seashells.

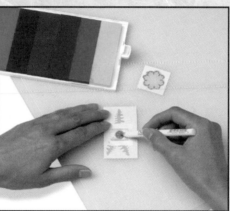

Stenciling Use the negative piece—the piece that's left over once you punch—as a stencil for chalking or sponge painting. Stencils can also be used as a template with a stylus for dry embossing on vellum.

Stitching Punch tiny holes on cardstock with a needle to mark where you want to place either hand- or machine-stitching. Practice with a sewing machine on scrap cardstock before stitching art.

Adding eyelets Punch a ¼" hole for eyelet. Insert eyelet; flip eyelet and paper over. Place pointed-end of setter into protruding end of eyelet. Tap setter with hammer; remove setter. Tap eyelet top again to complete the set.

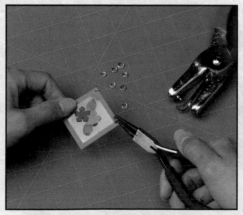

Adding jewelry-making components Punch a tiny hole in paper; insert jump ring and close loop with needle-nose pliers. Use jump rings to connect eyelets or to dangle charms from punch art.

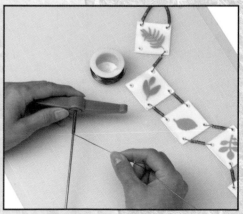

Adding wire Make spirals with a wire wrapping tool or skewer. Use needle-nose pliers to help twist, bend and pinch wire into shapes; adhere with adhesive or insert wire end through paper and secure on back with tape.

Red

Red, the king of primary colors, is the flashiest and most dramatic color of the spectrum. Its passion and vitality will add spice to your punch art designs. We can't think of red without thinking of Valentine's Day, Christmas and just plain, flashy fun! In nature, the rich red petals of the rose are set off by dark green leaves, making these colors the perfect complement for each other. Deep reds—like burgundy, maroon and wine—add a timeless elegance to punch art. Its softer shades of pink, the sweetest of colors, remind us of dainty blossoms and gentle femininity. Bright shades of red and hot pink can seem overpowering and demanding on the scrapbook page, but when used in small doses, these shades are striking and not harsh. Go cheery. Go bold. Go red!

(left)
See page 86 for punches
and products used.

Decorate Torn Mulberry Ribbon

Punch art patterns can go on just about anything! For a wrapped present with homespun appeal, accent torn strips of mulberry paper "ribbon" with $5/16$" circles, small quasars (Emagination Crafts) and geometric shapes from the uppercase alphabet kit (Family Treasures).

Add Texture With Wire

Enhance the texture of punch art on a scrapbook page with craft wire, which is available in different colors and gauges. Wire can be hand-shaped into letters, words or fun design elements. Mount matted and single photos. Adhere upper and lower borders, cut from complementary-colored paper, to page. Accent borders with negative pieces from swirl border punch and $5/8$" circles (both Family Treasures). Add hand-shaped wire (Artistic Wire) spirals. Finish with freehand cut and lettered title banner and journaling.

Photos Pennie Stutzman

Accent a Handmade Stocking

A punch art and beaded vellum stocking makes a fun container for little surprise gifts or a useful page pocket for holding holiday letters. Enlarge and photocopy the pattern on page 89 onto two sheets of vellum; cut out. Add complementary-colored eyelets (Impress Rubber Stamps; see technique on page 17) to outer edges. Freehand cut strips of paper for bands; adhere strips, gluing beaded fringe beneath lower strip. Accent band with $3/16$" small circle, small diamond, chain link, small sun (all EK Success), $1 5/16$" circle (Family Treasures) and sequins (Westrim).

The Rendon Family

These are our first family photos since Tiana was 2. She's now 9 and Travis is 12. Good thing Randy and I never age! October, 2000.

Combine Decorative Elements With Style

Enrich a natural photo setting with elegant, deep-colored decorative elements. Follow the punch progression steps to the right to create floral medallions, using 1½" squares, super giant circles, dot mini extension (all Family Treasures) and a petal leaf (EK Success) in coordinating colors. Add eyelets (Impress Rubber Stamps; see technique on page 17); mount floral medallions on squares. Assemble page with medallions, patterned paper (Keeping Memories Alive) strips, matted photos and journaling and title blocks. *Jenna Beegle, Photos Shawna Rendon*

Make a Monochromatic Montage

A collection of punched shapes in varying shades of one color invites the eye to see the whole picture, rather than focus on one specific area. Begin by building the design from the bottom up, mounting the largest punched shapes first and filling in spaces with smaller, detailed shapes. This montage uses a large swirl border punch and large and small spirals (all Family Treasures), giant dragonflies (McGill), negative pieces from leaf border (All Night Media), ⅛" round circles and small teardrops (Fiskars). Experiment with different arrangements and punched shapes for your own unique, tone-on-tone montage. *Valerie Brincheck, Ann Kitayama*

One Punch

Primitive Heart

Maximize your return on punch investments by challenging yourself to create as many border patterns as possible with just one punch. On pages 31, 40, 41, 47, 55, 65, 73 and 83, you'll see more smart examples of border patterns created using a single punch. Start with a basic border and slowly work your way up to more elaborate designs. Play around with the arrangement to create striking new patterns. Experiment with printed, velvet or metallic papers; jewelry-making components (see technique on page 17); beads; sequins and more for subtle or dramatic variations of each new border design. *Kelly Angard, Jenna Beegle*

For a simple, lighthearted motif, alternate solid and patterned paper (Colors by Design) hearts horizontally and vertically, equal distances apart.

An unabashedly wild pattern starts with a foursome of patterned paper (Keeping Memories Alive, Making Memories) hearts whose lower tips touch at center. Add center heart on foam spacer for height.

This broken-hearted pattern is assembled with three hearts as shown, topped with a fourth suede paper (Nag Posh) heart sliced down the middle with decorative scissors (Fiskars).

Make a flashy, topsy-turvy pattern by alternating solid-colored and metallic paper (Making Memories) hearts alternately right side up and upside down, equal distances apart, aligning upper and lower edges to form a straight line. Accent with beads layered atop sequins for pizazz.

Create a chained melody by linking punched hearts and patterned paper (The Crafter's Workshop) quasars (both Emagination Crafts) together with jump rings (Halcraft) used for making jewelry (see page 17).

Punch Stamped or Printed Images

Simple shapes, punched from stamped designs or clip art printed on colored paper, create imaginative visuals. Stamp images (sun, Rubber Stampede; clock, Rubber Stamps of America) on paper. Add dimension without bulk by heat-embossing stamped image before punching, if desired. Flip large primitive heart (Emagination Crafts) and medium hand (Family Treasures) punches over and position stamped images as desired; punch images off-center in the punch as shown for a contemporary look. Mount punched shapes on corrugated paper (DMD Industries) with self-adhesive foam spacers and faceted stones for depth. *Pamela Frye*

Add Passion With Glass Marbles

Embellish squares, repunched with hearts, with bright, tiny glass marbles (Halcraft) for passionate appeal. Begin with patterned paper (Design Originals) background covered with vellum (Hot Off The Press) for color. Add double-matted photos, border strip and journaling block. Punch a heart (Family Treasures) from double-sided mounting adhesive (Therm O Web). Flip square punch (Family Treasures) over; insert and center negative heart and repunch. Peel backing from square and adhere to paper. Remove backing from positive heart; place on paper in center of square. Peel top backing from heart; press red glass marbles into place. Peel top backing from square as shown and press purple glass marbles into place. *Pamela Frye, Photos Shelley Balzer*

Slice Shapes for a Colorful Collage

A creative collage of numbers or letters, sliced and reassembled (see page 17), provides an interactive and playful background element. Follow the punch progression steps below and punch numbers (Family Treasures) in coordinating colors. Randomly reassemble the pieces for a multicolored effect. Mount beneath and atop photos and title blocks. *Pam Klassen, Photos Angie McGoveran*

2222

Stitch Some Homespun Stripes

A happy, abstract pattern of multiple stripes, stitching, cross-stitching and leaves creates a border with homespun appeal. First, cut stripes to fit page from cardstock colors of choice. Punch large birch leaves (Family Treasures). Punch small oak leaves (HyGlo/AmericanPin); repunch oak leaves with medium birch leaf punch. Assemble—but do not adhere—your stripes and leaves in the pattern that you like best. Follow the steps below to apply stitching by hand, then assemble and adhere border to page. *Kathleen Aho, Jenna Beegle*

1 *Draw dots on cardstock stripes and large birch leaves with a pencil where you want stitching to be (see page 17). Hand punch 1/16" holes over dots (Figure 1) or pierce dots with a sewing needle.*
2 *Align cardstock stripes and stitch together as desired, using three strands of embroidery floss and a sewing needle (Figure 2). For variation, alternate straight stitches, cross-stitches, zig-zag stitches, etc. on different stripes.*
3 *Stitch leaves prior to mounting cardstock stripes on page (Figure 3).*

Create Dimension With Layers

Autumn leaves take on new texture with the added dimension of layering (see page 16) with self-adhesive foam spacers. To create the border design here, punch twelve super jumbo rectangles (Nankong); mount on side of patterned background paper (Creative Imaginations). Punch two sets of leaves in the following shapes in large and jumbo: oak, white oak, grapevine leaf, ivy, hawthorn (all Emagination Crafts) and birch (Family Treasures). Layer smaller leaf over larger leaf with ⅛" foam spacer (3M) and then again on coordinating rectangle with foam spacer. *Valerie Brincheck, Photos Katherine T. Hilton*

Use Punched Shape to Emboss

Get more from your punches by using the punched shapes for patterns or templates to "emboss" vellum. This quick-and-easy technique can be used with most any punch shape and vellum color when a light and airy—and sometimes dainty—impression is needed. Begin with a solid-colored background that is darker than your vellum. Then follow the steps to the right to create an embossed vellum overlay on which you will mount matted photos, title and journaling blocks. Add extra embossed shapes for accent, if desired. *Alison Beachem*

1 Punch giant flower (Family Treasures) from dark cardstock for easier viewing beneath vellum. Add white punched ¾" circle (Marvy/Uchida) at flower's center (Figure 1) to complete your "pattern."

2 Place punched pattern beneath vellum along vellum's lower edge, beginning on the left. Use an embossing stylus to partially trace around the pattern. Shift pattern a little down and to the right, allowing it to overlap the tracing you just did. Partially trace pattern again. Repeat this step, moving pattern farther to the right and up and down as needed to complete the design (Figure 2).

3 Use sharp scissors to cut away lower edge of vellum to form lacy edge (Figure 3). If desired, add cardstock strips beneath top and sides of vellum overlay, cardstock circles beneath vellum at center of flowers and extra embossed accents on page for a polished look.

An Egg'stra Special Easter

We dyed them, and then found them
Savannah 1997

Slice a Mosaic Border

Add a captivating look to simple pages with a mosaic border panel overlaid with vellum for visual intrigue. Start with a matted background and photo. Adhere four large squares (Family Treasures) evenly spaced on a 2½" wide strip of cardstock. Stack four medium squares (Family Treasures) of different colored papers and use a metal straightedge ruler and craft knife to slice and reassemble (see page 17) them; mount on large squares. Attach vellum strip (The Paper Company) over panel with eyelets (Stamp Studio; see technique on page 17). *Joan Gosling*

Reproduce Elements From Photos

Reproducing elements from a photo in punch art is an effective way to create harmony and dimension. Here, dainty, pearl-accented flowers harmonize beautifully with the fancy dress and hat of the little girl in the photo. On patterned background (Sonburn) add small primitive hearts (Emagination Crafts) and mini birch leaves (Marvy/Uchida) at evenly spaced intervals as shown. Accent flowers and leaves with pearlessence glitter glue (Art Institute) and tiny pearls (Westrim). Add double-matted photo and title block trimmed with ribbon (Offray), strung pearls (Scrappy's Magic Scraps) and handmade floral bead accent. *Liane Smith*

Add Pen Stroke Details

It's easy to add relief details to a soft, layered floral border with just a few strokes of a pen. Begin with a matted 1½" border strip. Then, using a ⁵⁄₁₆" circle, a large daisy and a fine black pen, follow the punch progression steps below to create the border's floral medallions. Mount floral medallions and small water drops (EK Success) alternately and evenly spaced to complete border. *Jenna Beegle*

Orange

Orange is the color of fiery autumn leaves, terra cotta pots and vibrant sunsets. It also reminds us of Halloween and Thanksgiving. Some neutral orange shades can help create a bold, retro feel; spicy, earthen orange shades lend themselves well to Eastern-influenced patterns. Deep oranges set off neutrals with pizazz. Citrus orange shades can add excitement to your page, and soft peach shades add a sense of peacefulness.

This secondary color, made up of red and yellow, makes an uplifting statement when used as a background or as an accent. Whichever shades of orange you choose, they will bring a warm robustness to your punch art designs.

(left)
See page 86 for punches
and products used.

Accent Small Trinket Boxes

Put a playful touch on cardboard photo trinket boxes, widely available at craft stores. Begin by covering boxes and lids in patterned (FLAX San Francisco) and solid-colored papers. Accent lids with small primitive hearts (Emagination Crafts), mini diamonds (All Night Media), mini square sequins (Scrappy's Magic Scraps), small rectangles and mini circles (EK Success), and beads (Westrim). Accent sides of boxes with checkers (EK Success), small squares (Carl) and bead-accented mini ovals (Family Treasures). *Photos Sylvie Abecassis & Mark Lewis*

Add Texture to an Album Cover

Punch art makes a bold statement when peeking through the photo slot of an album (Kolo) cover. Begin with a 3½" square of cardstock for background. Cut assorted patterned (FLAX San Francisco) and solid-colored papers into graduated sizes of triangles; layer on background and trim off any overhang at edges. Add checkers (EK Success), small squares (Carl) and sliced daisies (Family Treasures) in pattern shown; mount on triangular background. Insert and center art into photo slot on album cover. Add album title in gold ink.

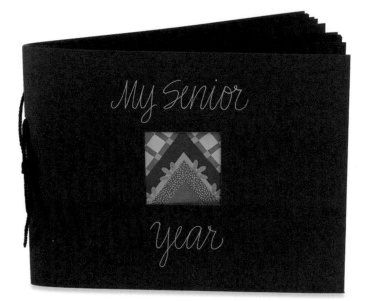

Trim Photo Mats With Flair

Use punched shapes to trim the edges of photo mats and pages for visual interest. Crop, mat and adhere photos on patterned background (Scrapbook Wizard). Decorate page edges with sliced flowers (EK Success), teardrops (McGill) and dots (Emagination Crafts). Accent photo mats with small building blocks (Family Treasures), hand-punched diamonds (McGill), sliced small circles, cones and dashes (all EK Success). Add title and journaling blocks. *Photos Mark Duncan*

One Punch

Buttercup

The small buttercup punch is a versatile punch that works well for creating retro-look border designs. Its semicircular shape can be arranged in a myriad of ways for a different pattern each time. An added bonus is the ⅛" round circle that is punched every time you punch the moon; experiment with incorporating it into your finished design, or replace the circle with a craft supply, such as a bead or a mini fastener.

Kelly Angard, Pam Klassen

EK Success' small buttercup punch was used to create our border patterns. Try any of the larger or smaller crescent moon and circle punches available for many different border pattern results.

Make a powerful pattern with moons punched from subtly patterned paper (FLAX San Francisco) and mounted as shown. Add gold ³⁄₁₆" mini deco fasteners (HyGlo/AmericanPin) to lower edge of punched moon border.

Start with a simple, playful pattern of punched moons, assembled to form a pinwheel. Add a punched circle at pinwheel center.

For a symmetrical reflection, mount a double row of similarly shaded moons with the tips facing inward as shown. Adhere the punched circles in the center of opposite-colored moons.

This pattern creates harmony in two ways: first, by using two different shades of the same color and second, by arranging the moons and circles in a yin-yang (opposite but always complementary) pattern.

Use negative space creatively for this oh-so-mystic border. Punch a 1" strip of paper at evenly spaced intervals; discard resulting positive shapes. Add colored papers to backside of the paper strip prior to mounting on page.

Create Raised Relief and Shadows

Look what a few simple slices and reassembly with double-sided, self-adhesive foam spacers can do to bring relief and shadows to your punch art! For this design, begin with a double-matted jumbo square at center, flanked at the four corners with double-matted small squares (all Family Treasures). Then follow the steps below to create the sliced detail on leaves. *Jenna Beegle*

1 *For corner leaf accents, punch 16 medium birch leaves (Family Treasures), eight from a light-colored paper, eight from a darker paper. Use a sharp craft knife to carefully slice "veins" into the lighter leaves (Figure 1; see technique on page 17). Mount atop darker leaves and adhere at corners of design.*
2 *Punch one large birch leaf (Family Treasures) from lighter paper and one from darker paper; mount darker leaf in center of jumbo square. Use a sharp craft knife to carefully slice apart the lighter leaf into six pieces (Figure 2).*
3 *Cut ⅛" thick foam spacers (Ranger Industries) in half or thirds. Reassemble leaf pieces, leaving ⅛" of space between the leaf pieces for added depth; mount atop lower leaf using foam spacer pieces (Figure 3).*

Accent a Photo Mat

Repetitious punch art borders become framed art
when used to accent photo mats. For an 11 x 14"
mat, link five 2¼" squares (Family Treasures) together with a 1¼" strip of adhered, complementary-
colored paper; embellish with pen stroke doodling
in gold ink. Accent border strip with ferns (The
Punch Bunch) and squares with negative pieces
from swirl border punch (Emagination Crafts).
Kathleen Childers, Photo Mark Lewis

Embellish a Classic Paisley Design

Add elegance to any page with timeless paisley designs.
Photocopy the patterns (see page 89), trace onto paper of choice
and cut out. Accent paisley with two
sizes of diamonds from a three-
diamond (McGill) and five-diamond
(Family Treasures) corner punch. Add
splashes (EK Success) to tail of paisley;
layer with diamonds. Accent inner
paisley with negative pieces from heritage border punch and large and
medium flowers (all Family Treasures);
layer with mini flowers (Family
Treasures) and negative pieces of five-
flower corner punch (McGill). Accent
outer edges of large paisleys with ¼"
circles layered with colored beads
(Westrim). Mount paisleys on page.
Add matted photo, hand-drawn title
and journaling to complete. *Valerie
Brincheck, Photo Ken Trujillo*

Photos on layout: SAN FRAN '71

Mom and
Dad loved to walk
in San Francisco and
take photos wherever they went.

Layer a Groovy Background

Re-create a visual "blast from the past" with a retro squares-turned-to-diamonds background for '70s photos. Add double-sided self-adhesive to sheets of vellum prior to punching. Punch, layer and mount various-sized squares (Family Treasures) in a diagonal diamond pattern across page to create background. Add matted and cropped photos on large, freehand cut squares. Cut and outline title letters using a lettering template (Starry Night Creations); mount with self-adhesive foam spacers. Finish with journaling on a triangle of vellum.

Valerie Brincheck, Photos Pamela Frye

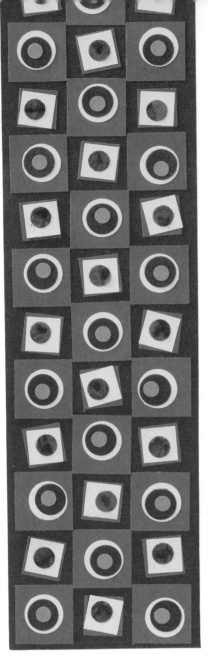

Punch Some Visual Intrigue

Various geometric shapes join forces to create a psychedelic pattern that complements photos. Note how the negative spaces between the octagons form squares to embellish or leave blank, if desired. Begin with a black background. Adhere various sizes of matted octagons cut from templates (Family Treasures, C-Thru Ruler Co., Paper Adventures) on page, arranged to create squares in negative space; trim octagons that overlap page edges. Add cropped photos and journaling to four center octagons. With tweezers in hand and patience at heart, work from the center square outward to embellish remaining octagons and squares with various sizes of small punched circles in patterns shown or patterns of your own choosing.
Kelly Angard, Photos Pam Klassen

Mix Geometric Shapes for Pizazz

When layered askew, simple geometric shapes add zip to border designs. Begin by adhering large squares in a checkerboard pattern. Layer the medium, small and mini circles in coordinating colors off-center on large squares. Fill the negative space of checkerboard in playful fashion with medium and small squares and ⁵⁄₁₆" circles (all Family Treasures).
Alison Beachem

Yellow

Yellow, the universal communicator, reminds us of sunny days filled with cheerfulness and warmth. We often equate a color with its origin in nature. For example, yellow is reminiscent of gardens full of daffodils and happy summer weddings. Color on paper is no different. Yellow is the perfect paper color choice for punch art designs that accent garden, summery and outdoor wedding photos. In golden shades, this outgoing color becomes quite regal. The optimistic attitude of bright yellows can be a bit overstimulating; but when used sparingly, these shades can make scrapbook pages appear larger. When combined with the stark contrast of deep blues, yellow commands attention. Soft and pale champagne yellows lend themselves well to heritage pages. Wherever you use yellow in your punch art designs, it's guaranteed to raise the spirits and bring a sense of joy!

(left)
See page 86 for punches
and products used.

Encase Multidimensional Punch Art

Protect a multidimensional punch art photo mat by encasing it in an acrylic frame. First, make a triple mat of monochromatic and complementary-colored papers, measured and trimmed to fit frame (Image Matters). Adhere layers together with self-adhesive foam spacers. Decorate mat with rows of mini extension squares and mini and small triangles (all Family Treasures). *Photo Ken Trujillo*

Trim Photos With Punch Art

Trimming photos with lightly accented punch art is a simple way to enhance photos without stealing their spotlight. Freehand cut and trim strips of paper to form diagonal page border and upper and lower edges of photo.

Accent strips with the following shapes punched from complementary-colored papers: small diamond, small building block (both Family Treasures), extended reach quasar (Emagination Crafts) and mini square (Family Treasures); mount on page. Arrange and adhere photos and additional punch art strips to page. Add title and journaling block. *Photos Joyce Feil*

Pen Stroke Outlines for Whimsy

Add a touch of lightheartedness with simple pen and marker strokes—a technique that works well with any punched shape—whenever a little dimension without added bulk is desired. Note how the two shades of ink create depth in the design. Begin with triple-matted background of solid and patterned papers (Provo Craft). Add matted photos and title block, then follow the steps below to outline punched jumbo clouds (Nankong), repunched super jumbo circle to create crescent moon, and various stars (EK Success, Family Treasures) with pen strokes. *Alison Beachem*

 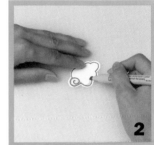

1 *Start with a pen stroke swirl in black ink (EK Success) that continues on to outline the clouds (Figure 1).*
2 *Trace over black line with gray brush marker (EK Success) to create shadow effect (Figure 2). Punch moon and stars from yellow paper. Outline in black; trace outer edges with orange marker.*

Make a Playful Frame

Display a playful collection of colorful flowers—punched from a variety of shapes in similar color intensities—to frame a photo or border an entire page. To make flowers, punch a number of garden flowers, daisies, flowers, pompoms and stars and layer with various-sized circles (all EK Success) in coordinating colors. *Alison Beachem, Photo Cynthia Anning*

Two Punches

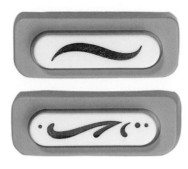

Family Treasures' swirl border punches #1 and #2, available only in the Swirl Punch Kit, were used to create our border patterns. Try other border punch combinations for endless design possibilities.

Swirl Borders

Occasionally, the negative shapes that fall from two different border punches work together in perfect harmony—like the similarly graceful designs of two swirl border punches. Experiment with the arrangement of the negative shapes from these punches to create your own flowing patterns that feature one or both punched designs.

Kelly Angard, Jenna Beegle, Michele Gerbrandt

Delicate meets bold when swirls are layered in an "X" and joined by ½" velvet circles layered with ¼" gold circles.

Overlap and alternate both border designs in a horizontal line for an elegantly understated pattern.

Place monochromatic-colored swirls end-to-end to mimic delicate, streaming ribbon.

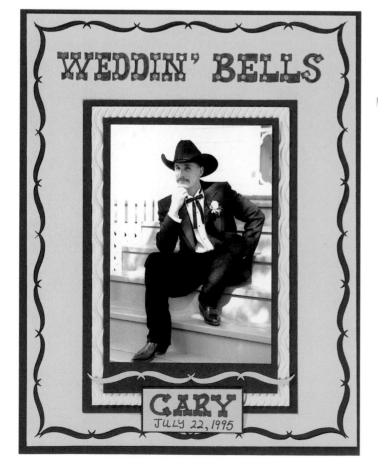

Twist a Barbed Wire Mat

Delicate meets sharp when this simple swirl border is used to successfully mimic twisted barbed wire. Begin with light-colored cardstock, cut to desired size. Flip border punch over; insert paper as far in as it will go beginning at one corner and punch. Overlap and punch repeatedly in a continuous design around the mat's edge until design is complete and the outside piece is separate from the inside piece. Mount on dark background. Add triple-matted photo, freehand drawn title and caption block to finish.

Alison Beachem, Photo Janet Voeller of Hot Off The Press

For an intricate looking, oh-so-easy pattern, first adhere darker vellum shapes in arrangement that is shown. Overlay and adhere lighter vellum shapes in opposite direction.

Use the concept of "reverse imaging" by adhering the positive pieces that fall from the border punch to create striking, reflective patterns with both border punches.

Interlock alternating-colored swirls for an interesting visual contrast.

Punch exquisite tone-on-tone contrast using monochromatic metallic and velvet papers.

Make a splash by placing the border punch's tiny negative pieces in between every set of back-to-back swirls, repeating until pattern is desired length.

These delicate beauties aren't for the faint of heart; it takes patience to arrange and assemble those tiny negative pieces, but the results are rewarding!

Use Negative Piece for Stencil

Another fun way to extend a punch's versatility is to use the negative piece—the piece that is left over after you punch your paper—as a stencil for chalking or sponge painting. It's the perfect punch solution when you need the brilliant drama of a watercolor border or scene to accent photos. These stencils can also be used with an embossing stylus for dry embossing on vellum (see page 26). To make a similar page, add strips of torn cardstock (Paper Adventures) to background. Mount silhouette-cropped and matted photos and journaling block. Cut 1½ x 2⅝" light-colored cardstock rectangles and then follow the steps to the right to "stencil" with your punches. *Beth Rogers, Photos Cheryl Rooney*

1 *Punch large trees (McGill) and silhouette flowers (Family Treasures) from squares of cardstock. Use removable artists tape to tape positive flower and resulting negative tree stencil onto cardstock rectangle in arrangement shown. The positive flower will remain in place as a "mask" while you move tree stencil around to ink "leaves." Apply green ink (Clearsnap) with applicator (Tsukineko). Repeat for two more leaves (Figure 1); remove leaf stencil and flower mask.*

2 *Tape negative flower stencil in center of leaves and apply light yellow ink to flower, then dab petal edges with orange ink (Figure 2); remove stencil.*

3 *Tape positive flower mask over stenciled flower again and add dark orange ink to center dots (Figure 3); remove stencil. If desired, color remaining positive flowers and trees to use for accent.*

Lydia *and* Derek

It was a beautiful morning ceremony held on the deck of the Willow Ridge Manor, with the reception following inside. I thought yellow was a happy, summer color to choose for bridesmaids' dresses, flowers and decorations.

Layer Vellum for Embossed Look

Soften a repetitive design with a vellum overlay, giving depth to your page with an embossed look. The vertical vine and leaf rows provide a lovely and simple pattern that doesn't take attention away from treasured photos. First, lightly draw vertical lines 1½" apart on background in pencil to use as a placement guide. Follow punch progression steps above to mount negative pieces from large vine border punch (Family Treasures) on pencil lines to create one row; repeat to cover background. Punch and adhere petal leaves (EK Success) on vine as shown. After completing rows, erase any remaining pencil marks and add vellum overlay. Mount matted photos, accented with additional punch art; journaling block and title to complete the page. *Jenna Beegle, Photos Lydia Rueger*

Join Shapes to Create New One

Extend your punches' versatility by experimenting with combined shapes. Here, a mega twig and a jumbo swirl (both Nankong) join together to create a filigree background. Note how the use of monochromatic papers, for both background and punched shapes, is another great way to mimic the look of embossed paper. Beginning in center of background paper, follow the punch progression steps below and cover background. Trim off overlapping designs at page's edges. Frame page with ¼" strips of paper. Mat title block and double-mat photo using paper and vellum; adhere to background. Add two punched designs to lower edge of photo to complete. *Alexandra Bleicher, Photos Harald Thonigs*

Renate nee Thonigs & Dieter Steigler
June 1967

Green

Nature's neutral—green—forms the refreshing, cool and shady back-drop of earth's gorgeous plants and flowers. A secondary color, made up of blue and yellow, green reminds us of new growth and new beginnings. As witnessed in nature, green provides a good balance of harmony to just about any other color. Deep greens—which lend a formal style to punch art—are perfect as accent colors with white, gray, yellow and cream-colored hues. Pale shades of green team well with pastel colors for a soft, romantic feel; shades of sage green offer a time-worn touch that is perfect for heritage photos. One of the most versatile hues on the color wheel, easy-going green makes all other colors turn green with envy.

(left)
See page 87 for punches
and products used.

Tag...You're It!

Make a personal statement on gift packages with handmade tags accented with punch art. Freehand cut tag. Adhere two layered medium and small circles at top; punch through both circles at once with a ³⁄₁₆" circle punch (EK Success) to create hole. Apply strips of colored paper to other end of tag; embellish with small triangles, mini squares, mini extension dots and mini diamonds (all Family Treasures). Add names, loop cord through hole and attach tag to gift.

Add Cheer to Holiday Ornaments

Clear glass ornaments, available at craft stores during the holidays, provide a clever showcase for punch art—whether the art is adhered to the outside or the inside of the ornament with tweezers. First, cut a narrow strip of paper for borders. Accent strips with mini swirls (Family Treasures) or halved water drops (EK Success) and star sequins. Fill ornaments with tinsel for a sparkly background.

Capture Riveting Moments

Punch art goes masculine with the addition of metallic fasteners, which are available in many colors, shapes and sizes. Begin with narrow border strips adhered in the shape of a diamond for background; embellish with mini ovals and dots (Family Treasures). Double-mat photos, pierce tiny hole in mat with needle and attach to background with deco fasteners (HyGlo/AmericanPin). Finish page with matted title lettering (C-Thru) and journaling block. *Photos MaryJo Regier*

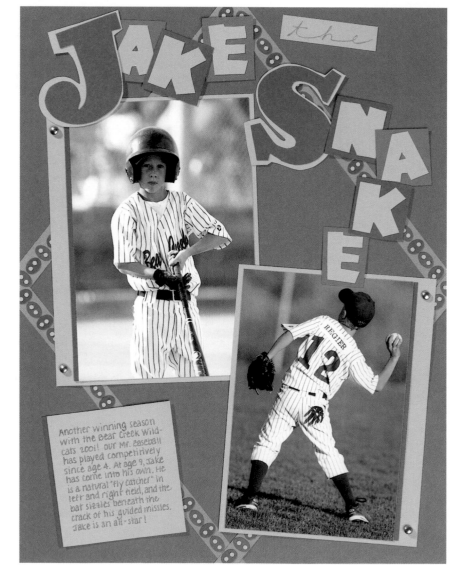

Another winning season with the Bear Creek Wildcats 2001! Our Mr. Baseball has played competitively since age 4. At age 9, Jake has come into his own. He is a natural "fly catcher" in left and right field, and the bat sizzles beneath the crack of his guided missles. Jake is an all-star!

One Punch

Diamond

The pointed tips of this simple geometric shape can be arranged in endless ways for a different result each time. Here, patterned papers, beads and sequins, eyelets, and metallic embroidery thread were used to help create our variations. Try new arrangements and other craft supplies shown on pages 14-15 for your own unique results. *Kelly Angard, Jenna Beegle*

EK Success' small diamond punch was used to create these border patterns. Larger and smaller diamond punches will allow you to change the scale of your design.

This simple diamond flower begins with a foursome of diamonds whose tips meet in the center. Beads and sequins are added for texture.

Squint your eyes to see that the horizontal center of this border begins with a continuous line of end-to-end diamonds. Then simply add six additional diamonds at evenly spaced intervals to form a floral pattern. Squint again and you'll see the *Ohio Star* quilt pattern in the negative space surrounding each center diamond.

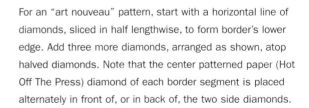

To achieve a simple, argyle-like pattern, mount three overlapped diamonds horizontally onto a vertical diamond as shown. Repeat until border is complete.

For an "art nouveau" pattern, start with a horizontal line of diamonds, sliced in half lengthwise, to form border's lower edge. Add three more diamonds, arranged as shown, atop halved diamonds. Note that the center patterned paper (Hot Off The Press) diamond of each border segment is placed alternately in front of, or in back of, the two side diamonds.

Here's another border that begins with a continuous, horizontal line of end-to-end diamonds. Gold eyelets (Impress Rubber Stamps; see technique on page 17) and metallic embroidery thread (DMC Corp.) are used to link vertical diamonds at the border's center, while foam spacers elevate vertical diamonds on both border ends for added dimension.

Create Shadows With Vellum

Combining two punched strips of vellum, layered and mounted askew, creates a shadowy, yet soft and sophisticated, border. The most visually appealing results come from using monochromatic strips of vellum paper (Paper Adventures), with the lighter shade on top and the darker shade beneath. Punch twine border (Marvy/Uchida) along lower edge of light-colored (top) vellum strip. Layer strips with darker one on bottom and lighter one on top; tape together with removable tape. Draw evenly spaced guidelines (see page 16) or "tick marks" on back of lighter vellum strip for punch placement accuracy. Follow the steps to the right to finish. *Jenna Beegle*

1 *Flip ash leaf punch (The Punch Bunch) over. Note: Applying double-sided self-adhesive to vellum strips will make it difficult to punch through both layers simultaneously. Insert and align taped-together vellum, placing marks where center of punch should be (Figure 1). Punch through layers until border is complete; erase marks.*

2 *Mount dark vellum strip on page with a drop of liquid adhesive at each corner. Repeat with lighter vellum strip, mounting askew atop dark vellum strip (Figure 2).*

Slice a Geometric Design

When sliced and reassembled, punched geometric shapes create interesting new patterns. For this border, punch 1½" circles and layer with 1" circles (both Marvy/Uchida) from contrasting or complementary-colored papers. Slice layered circles into quarters; reassemble into half circle designs. Punch and layer 1⁵⁄₁₆" and ⅝" squares in like fashion. Assemble elements as shown; adhere to page and trim off any overlap at page's edge. For added dimension, layer elements with self-adhesive foam spacers. Try cropping photos into circles and squares to complement border design, if desired. *Jenna Beegle*

Make an Artsy, Free-Form Pattern

Fashion a free-flowing art deco design out of vibrantly colored, repunched circle rings; leaves; sequins and faceted stones. When repunching (see page 16), start with smaller-sized punch. First punch large circle (Family Treasures). Flip extra large circle punch (Family Treasures) over, insert and center punched paper; repunch to form rings. Punch ash leaves (Martha Stewart). Randomly mount rings and leaves on card. Accent card with ¼" punched circles, faceted stones and sequins for texture. *Erikia Ghumm*

Sarah in the Summer
august ♥ 2000

the flowers were taller than you that year!

String a Daisy Chain Frame

Recapture a touch of youth with this punched daisy chain frame, made soft with pastel papers and playful eyelets for the daisies' centers. Mount photo in center of cardstock background. Encircle photo with punched border swirl (Family Treasures) to create "vine." Fasten eyelets (Impress Rubber Stamps; see page 17) to small daisies (EK Success); mount on vine with liquid adhesive. Place small folk hearts (EK Success) on vine. Add hand-drawn vine tendrils, title and journaling in pastel ink to finish. *Jenna Beegle*

Embellish Gift Tags

Create charming gift tags with punches, vellum, fabric, chalk and pens. Flip super jumbo primitive heart punch (Emagination Crafts) over, insert gift tags (Impress Rubber Stamps) one at a time, center heart and punch. For sheer heart, cut patterned vellum paper (Colorbök) larger than punched shape; adhere to back of tag. Pen detail of dots, hearts and lines around shape and edges of tag. Lightly chalk (Craf-T Products) over pen designs. For Victorian tag, use a needle to punch holes outlining heart. Hold a small patch of flat, fabric-covered batting behind tag; stitch (see page 17) in place and add button. Chalk around edges of tag; lightly dust with brown chalk for an aged look. *Helen Naylor*

for you

Hang a Pressed-Flower Glass Illusion

If you've admired the beauty of pressed
flowers sandwiched between two pieces
of leaded glass, then you'll love these
dainty little "punched glass" illusions.
One variation (right) hangs vertically
from a button and piece of hemp, its
panes connected by jump rings. The
other variation (below) hangs horizontally from knotted hemp and jump rings.
Follow the steps below to create the
version of choice. *Beth Rogers*

1 *Punch smaller 1¼" square first; adhere square to
uncut piece of clear film (Graphix). Repunch 1⁹⁄₁₆"
(Figure 1; see technique on page 16) with larger square
(both Family Treasures) through both layers to create
"glass frames."*
2 *Punch holes for jump rings (Figure 2) with a ¹⁄₁₆"
round hand punch (McGill) on all corners for vertically
hung art; only at top two corners for horizontally hung
art. Connect jump rings (see technique on page 17).*
3 *Punch small leaves and flowers (All Night Media,
EK Success, HyGlo/AmericanPin, Family Treasures)
from mulberry or vellum papers that have been backed
with double-sided self-adhesive for strength. Remove
backing; adhere flowers to "glass" (Figure 3).*

Press Leaves Under Vellum

"Press" real or punched leaves beneath vellum instead
of clear film and add wire (Artistic Wire) spirals and
eyelets for a rugged touch. Punch 1¼" squares (Family
Treasures) from white vellum and cardstock; sandwich
punched leaves (Emagination Crafts, Family Treasures,
Martha Stewart) or real pressed leaves between layers.
Add eyelets at corners; connect with wire spirals (see
both techniques on page 17). *Jenna Beegle*

Bend Wire Into a Border Design

Working fine gauge wire into your designs adds interest and texture to a repetitive border pattern. Begin by punching large ivy leaves (Emagination Crafts) from handmade paper. Cut 24-gauge wire (Artistic Wire) into 1½" pieces; bend into swirls with pliers. Mount top part of leaf to page; before adhering stem portion, punch a small hole with a needle or safety pin and insert end of wire through to back of paper. Tape wire securely to back of page. Adhere stem of leaf over wire hole. Repeat to finish border. *Jenna Beegle*

Slice in Realistic Detail

Try the combination of slicing in detail and chalking accents to bring in a touch of realism. It's a great technique for punched shapes that are organic in nature—like leaves, flowers, trees and seashells. Begin with double-matted photo and nameplate. Follow the steps below to create a border, overlapping finished leaves as shown.

Jenna Beegle, Photo Pennie Stutzman

1 *Punch jumbo grapevine leaves (Emagination Crafts) from complementary-colored papers. Use a sharp craft knife to carefully slice in detail (see page 17) of "veins" onto the leaves.*
2 *Use a sponge-tip applicator to apply chalk (Craf-T Products) lightly to the edges of each leaf in a shade that is just a tiny bit darker than the paper.*

Blue

Blue—the color of our planet—is a cool hue that soothes and relaxes us as well as our scrapbook pages. It reminds us of the ocean's calming waves lapping at the shoreline and tranquil lakes frozen in time. And what is more optimistic than a bright blue sky? Many shades of blue together can intensify the color's chilliness—making blue shades a great choice for wintry snowflake designs. Red can balance blue's tendency to appear cold. On the other hand, cobalt, turquoise and aquamarine can heat up your punch art with electric vitality. Pale and dusty blues work well with soft pinks, greens and white when your photos require a delicate touch. A true chameleon, blue lends a calm, cool and collected inspiration to your punch art designs.

(left)
See page 87 for punches
and products used.

Dress Up Photos Beneath Glass

Punch art side borders are a snappy way to dress up photos under glass. Mount photos on patterned paper (Hot Off The Press). Cut paper side borders to fit frame using a decorative ruler. Accent border with ¾" squares (Family Treasures), pompoms, ¼" and ³⁄₁₆" circles (all EK Success) and sequins (Westrim). *Photos Ken Trujillo*

Add Beads for Dimension

Turn two-dimensional punch art into three-dimensional punch art with bead accents. Start with a matted border strip decorated with medium and small decorative squares (Family Treasures), shining star (EK Success), mini extension quasar (Emagination Crafts) and bugle beads (Westrim). Mount matted photos. Finish with title lettering (DJ Inkers) and journaling block mounted on torn mulberry paper mats and accented with mini quasars and beads. *Photos Nicole La Cour*

One Punch

Fleur-de-lis

Family Treasures' small fleur-de-lis punch was used to create our border patterns. Larger and smaller fleur-de-lis punches allow you to change the scale of your border design.

Here's a small sampling of the handsome border patterns that you can create with a small fleur-de-lis punch. The timeless, classic punch shape lends itself well to heritage scrapbook pages. Re-create our heraldic borders or make your own new ones by arranging the punched fleur-de-lis shapes into countless new configurations. It's easy!

Kelly Angard, Jenna Beegle

Arrange punched shapes into a foursome, with the sides touching and the lower points of the fleurs-de-lis pointed inward to form a traditional floral medallion pattern in the center. Use 1/16" round hand punch to add accents at corners and center of design.

This simple pattern consists of fleur-de-lis shapes adhered end-to-end, with each one offset a tiny bit as shown.

For a "clearly" regal border, mount punched shapes alternately, rightside up and upside down, overlapping the edges as shown. Use vellum for one of the papers to create a see-through effect.

Create a bold, brave border statement by lining up punched fleurs-de-lis on a strip of background paper. Add faceted stones (The Beadery) for dimension.

For a gallant medallion, arrange punched fleurs-de-lis into a foursome again, this time with the top of each fleur-de-lis touching at the center. Use 1/16" round hand punch to add accents at corners and center of design.

Make an imperial impression by overlapping and layering various-colored fleur-de-lis shapes as shown.

Jordan and Joshua had a blast playing in their new water fun pool. They fished, splashed and had themselves a good time all afternoon. August 2001

Add a New Twist With Wire

Add a new twist to punch art with hand-shaped wire words and textural design elements. For the photo frame, alternate medium triangles (The Punch Bunch) highlighted with chalks (Craf-T Products) and 24-gauge silver wire (The Beadery) twisted into scrolls. Adhere wire by leaving a ½" length at the end of wire design, slip into a small hole pierced in paper with a needle, and tape wire end to back of page to secure. For border, mark punch guidelines (see page 16) on back of 1½" wide strip of paper at 1¼" intervals. Insert border strip into upside-down, ¾" circle punch (Marvy/Uchida), center guideline marks and punch. Quarter slice positive circles, chalk and set aside. Punch a second set of circles, in coordinating color, slice one-third off of circle, chalk and mount along lower edge of border. Layer quartered circle slices atop two-thirds circles on border. Twist wires into swirls; adhere. Add wire title, matted photos and journaling to complete. *Alexandra Bleicher*

Contrast Bold With Soft

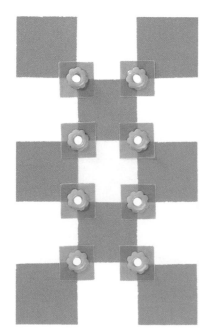

The frilly edge of a floral eyelet successfully counteracts the boldness of a linear, square design. Begin by mounting 2" squares (Family Treasures) punched from vellum in a three-column checkerboard pattern. Layer smaller 1³⁄₁₆" squares (Family Treasures) over points where two corners meet; add eyelets (Stampin FUNaddict; see technique on page 17). Flatten petals by placing towel over eyelets before hammering to "set" them. *Jenna Beegle*

Repunch a Stained-Glass Border

Use geometric-shaped punches to create beautiful stained-glass borders. Follow the steps below to create the border on a dark background. Then mount matted title, journaling blocks and photos and adhere additional stained-glass border patterns between photos to complete page. *Marty Mueller*

1 *Insert paper strip halfway into upside-down small circle punch (EK Success); punch and discard resulting semi-circles. Repunch paper strip over negative punched semi-circles (Figure 1; see technique on page 16) to make crescents that will flank whole circles in border design.*

2 *In the same manner, punch large rectangle (Family Treasures) and then repunch short end of rectangle with small circle punch (Figure 2), forming shape that will flank crescent shapes in border design. Punch small squares and cut some in half for small rectangles.*

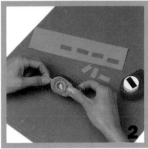

Assemble punched "glass" elements to create border design.

Punch a Quilted Border

Monochromatic-colored shapes, sliced and reassembled, make an intriguing hybrid—a cross between the *Lazy Daisy* and *Tumbling Blocks* quilt patterns. To make border, start with a 1½" strip of black paper. Punch 22 small building blocks (Family Treasures) from various shades of the same color; slice building blocks in half. Punch 22 small ⅜" squares from darker shade of same color family. Follow the punch progression steps below to assemble border, leaving ¹⁄₁₆" between the pieces for background to show through and slicing in half the squares along the edge of the border. Punch and assemble corner embellishments; adhere to double-matted photo. In the same manner, punch, assemble and adhere small border beneath photo and add matted title block to finish the page. *Valerie Brincheck*

Fashion an Amish Floral Frame

Frame a special photo with a simple composition, reminiscent of a traditional Amish design. Mount photo at center; frame with a Star of David (All Night Media) layered with a small daisy (Marvy/Uchida), mini flower and ⅛" circle. Use negative pieces from the baroque border punch (All Night Media) to fill spaces between flowers; adorn with mini hearts. Add matted title and journaling. *Jenna Beegle*

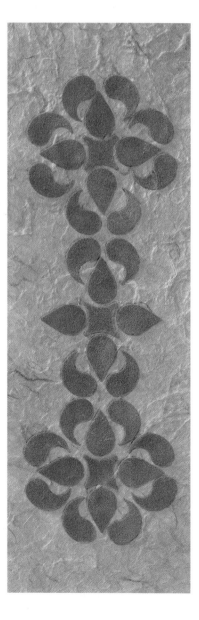

Show Off With Specialty Papers

An elegant, ornate design deserves the rich luxury of textured papers to showcase its beauty. Here, shapes are punched from velvet paper (Wintech) and mounted on mulberry paper. Begin design with a small quasar (Emagination Crafts) surrounded by four small water drops (EK Success). Elaborate with eight small splashes (EK Success) for the large design and four small splashes for the alternating small design. For added impact, accent the border with faceted stones, micro beads or sequins. *Jenna Beegle*

Repunch Argyle Squares

While this technique works well with many punches, repunching is particularly effective for creating a monochromatic, argyle look that perfectly accents heritage photos. Begin with matted background of patterned paper and solid-colored cardstock. Add double-matted photo and title block in center of page. Follow the steps below to create argyle border and corner accents. *Valerie Brincheck*

1 *Punch small, medium and large squares (Family Treasures) from shades of the same color of plaid patterned papers (All My Memories, Fiskars, Lasting Impressions), then repunch squares with giant and jumbo square punches (Figure 1) thus creating the design from the inside out. Layer and overlap argyle squares in border, photo and corner embellishments as shown; adhere.*

Slice and Reassemble a Mosaic

If photo mosaics seem too time-consuming to make, try this simple sliced and reassembled mosaic frame. Begin by mounting a trimmed 3½ x 5" photo onto a 6 x 7" piece of dark cardstock. Follow the punch progression steps below. For frame, punch fourteen 1" squares and four 1¼" squares (both Family Treasures). Snip a ½" right angle into one corner of each of the four larger corner squares as shown; mount on background leaving ¼" between squares and photo. Mount 1" squares in the same fashion. Punch medium (Emagination Crafts) and mini snowflakes in coordinating colors. Slice medium snowflakes; mount segments on mosaic squares as shown. Scatter mini snowflakes randomly; adhere. *Alison Beachem*

Punch a Dutch-Inspired Pattern

A graceful pattern, inspired by Dutch art, flows across the page. Draw two intersecting lines—one horizontal and one vertical—across back of page to mark center for placement of punched shapes. Draw more lines to create a grid of 2⅛" squares. Place page right side up on light box; adhere mini quasar (Emagination Crafts) at center to begin design. Follow the punch progression steps at left to assemble flowers using small water drop, splash (both EK Success) and mini teardrop (McGill). Hand slice ¹⁄₁₆ x 1" strips of paper for stems. Punch border swirls (Family Treasures); mount at stem bases. Add water drops by swirls. Repeat steps, making sure swirls meet from row to row. *Jenna Beegle*

Add Interest With Printed Papers

Printed papers add pizazz to simple punched art, no matter its shape or size. Create this fresh-looking design with a patterned paper (Hot Off The Press) by slicing a thin strip of printed paper for the center of the border. Punch seashells (Martha Stewart); adhere on opposite sides of strip. Border the design with mini circles (EK Success) placed about ⅛" apart. *Alison Beachem*

Use Punches and Piercing to Tat Lace

Magic happens in the form of delicate, ornamental lace when you combine vellum paper, a decorative lace corner punch, piercing and dangling beads. Begin with stamped (Impress Rubber Stamps) cardstock for background. Follow the steps at right to create lacy vellum overlay; adhere to background around top and side edges when finished. Add oval-cropped and matted photos hung from metallic embroidery thread and deco fasteners (HyGlo/AmericanPin). Add title block and journaling to complete. *Jenna Beegle, Photos Cheryl Rooney*

1 *Remove punch guides (see page 16) from a decorative lace corner punch (All Night Media). Flip punch over and insert light-colored vellum paper—as far in as it will go to ensure an evenly straight punched edge every time—and punch. Repeat as needed across lower edge of paper to create lacy punched edge (Figure 1).*
2 *Use a tiny heart hand punch (Fiskars) to repunch lace edge at evenly spaced intervals (Figure 2).*
3 *Use piercing tool and mat (Pergamano) to pierce vellum in a straight line (Figure 3) across edge. Pierce additional accents on lower edges of vellum, around corner punch designs, if desired.*
4 *Pierce center of lacy fringe created by corner punch for dangling beads. Thread a single strand of metallic embroidery floss (DMC Corp.) through holes one at a time (Figure 4), adding a bead (The Bead Shoppe); tie off ends to finish.*

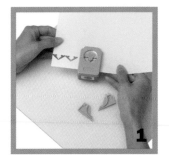

Repunch a Shadow Box

Make a simple yet intriguing "shadow box" border to highlight small, punched shapes or a portion of a photo. Begin with a 2¼" wide strip of paper for background. Punch smaller, medium square first. Flip super giant square punch over (both Family Treasures); insert punched paper. Position medium negative square in corner and repunch (see page 16). Adhere vellum to back of large squares; mount small tri leaf and lotus (both EK Success) and butterfly (Family Treasures) on vellum windows. *Joan Gosling*

Purple

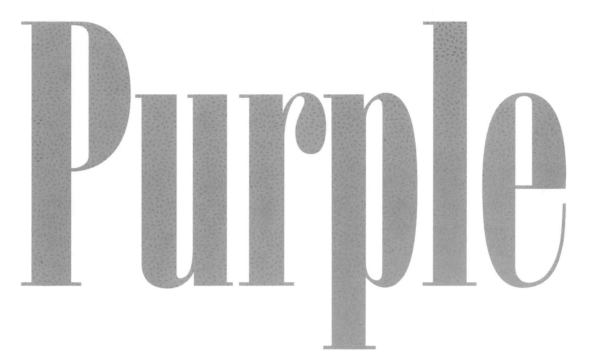

Purple, the noble gem of the color wheel, has been the color of royalty for centuries. The purple color family is a favorite of children of all ages. As an accent, the bright and deep purples and plums are great for adding splashes of sporty color to punch art designs. These dark purples are also a rich accent color with creams and ivories. Purple's lighter, softer shades of lavender and pale violet are ultra-feminine—perfect for "little girl" pages. Try infusing highlights of oranges and yellows to add zing to your mystical purple creations!

(left)
See page 87 for punches and products used.

Punch Up a Light Switch

Add form to function with a punch art switchplate! Use switchplate (Crafter's Pride) backing for pattern; transfer to corrugated paper (DMD Industries) for background. Accent with torn mulberry strips, flowers, swirls (both EK Success) and dots. Frame switch hole with negative shapes from photo mounting punch, northern star (both Emagination Crafts), sequins and beads. Assemble switchplate; install according to packaging instructions.

Present a United Front

Matted border strips, united with eyelets, provide a strong visual element to this scrapbook page. Begin by mounting photo, triple-matted with complementary-colored and torn parchment (Paper Adventures) papers, on patterned paper (Hot Off The Press) background. Freehand cut and layer border strips; add eyelets (Impress Rubber Stamps; see technique on page 17). Accent borders with small diamonds (EK Success) halved lengthwise; mount on background. Shade title lettering (DJ Inkers) on parchment paper, layer over torn and matted paper strip and secure with eyelets. Mount title block atop upper border and add journaling block to complete page.
Photo Dawn Mabe

One Punch

Daisy

Beloved for its playful and cheery rays, the daisy punch shows off its versatility. We illustrate just a few of the simple border patterns you can make with a daisy. For variation, try slicing apart the punched shape's petals and reassembling for new configurations. Experiment with patterned papers or add other craft supplies to make your daisies bloom! *Kelly Angard, Valerie Brincheck*

Carl's large daisy punch was used to create these border patterns. Larger, smaller and differently shaped daisies can be used for a myriad of new patterns and designs.

To make an oh-so-sweet daisy chain, punch daisies from shades of the same color of paper. Mount daisies evenly spaced, alternating each one to the left or right of the previous one to form the chain.

For subtle, two-tone trickery, punch daisies from solid- and complementary-colored patterned paper (Hot Off The Press). Halve daisies, slicing through two petals as shown. Reassemble daisies, joining one solid-colored half with one patterned half. Adhere on page, alternating every other daisy.

For another simple pattern, use a craft knife to "dissect" or slice off four of the daisy's petals. Mount dissected daisies as shown, adding a dissected and layered complete daisy every third time.

Create a close-knit daisy chain by interlocking solid and patterned paper daisies as shown.

Layer two shades of punched daisies and add a clear faceted stone at the center for a dainty, understated look.

Repunch a Baroque Border

Combine punched and repunched shapes to create a beautiful heritage border. Choose two complementary-colored papers—we chose a solid-colored and patterned paper (The Crafter's Workshop). For a 12 x 12" scrapbook page, cut a 1¾" wide border strip background from patterned paper. Embellish both long sides of the border strip using an oval border punch (Family Treasures); adhere. Follow the steps below to create the border design. *Alexandra Bleicher*

Make a Monochromatic Brocade Background

To create a beautiful brocade background, use a pencil to lightly draw an "X" to mark the center of the page. Begin with the large center medallion made up of one small quasar (Emagination Crafts) at the center, surrounded by a foursome of large fleurs-de-lis (McGill), small splashes and small teardrops (both EK Success). Repeat this medallion four more times, in the same color of paper, to create a cross pattern. Make four smaller, darker medallions using a foursome of large punched fleurs-de-lis joined at the lower tips with a small quasar. Mount medallions, spaced evenly next to the four arms of the cross as shown. Embellish each quasar with a faceted stone to complete the brocade background. *Jenna Beegle*

1 *Punch paper using baroque border punch (All Night Media); set the pieces that fall from punch aside for later use (Figure 1).*
2 *Flip a jumbo seashell punch (Martha Stewart) over, insert and center paper punched with baroque border; repunch with shell design as shown (Figure 2). Repeat with six remaining paper rectangles. Adhere resulting "tree" shapes and negative baroque border pieces, evenly spaced, along the length of the border to finish.*

THE VIEW FROM OUR COTTAGE

the cry of the loon is always so beautiful! I wait to hear from them each evening.

Mix Squares for Symmetrical Balance

The mix of monochromatic and printed vellum papers and various sizes of overlapped squares create a symmetrically unimposing and peaceful backdrop for this tranquil photo. Begin with patterned background (The Crafter's Workshop). Randomly overlap and adhere various-sized squares (Family Treasures) punched from patterned (all Hot Off The Press) and solid-colored vellum papers for page border. Add vellum-matted photo in center and journaling. *Chris Peters, Photo Thelma Molkoski*

Layer Squares Off-Center for Retro Boldness

Graduating sizes of squares, combined with dark and white papers, are layered off-center for a handsome, striking pattern. Begin with 1½" squares (Family Treasures) punched from two complementary colors of dark papers; adhere in a checkerboard pattern on white background. Layer 1¼", 1", ⅝", ¾", and ½" squares (all Family Treasures)—punched from each of the three colors—off-center to keep the three-dimensional design from looking too linear. Soften the design by either changing colors to muted hues or punching squares from patterned paper. *Jenna Beegle*

Add Sparkle to Seasonal Shapes

Snowflake designs—a work of art all their own—come to life with sparkly texture and dimension by punching a variety of snowflake shapes (Carl, HyGlo/AmericanPin, Emagination Crafts) and with adhesive glitter sheets (Ranger Industries) or glitter glue. Mat on giant square before layering on jumbo scalloped square (both Family Treasures). Enhance your seasonal layout by changing the colors to match a festive holiday photo. *Tracy Johnson*

Create Drama With Reverse Imaging

Reverse imaging creates a "positive/negative" effect, achieved by slicing two punched shapes, in different colors, at the same time and reassembling pieces into the original shape, lining up the different colored pieces. Start with a bi-color, four-square background. Punch super jumbo butterflies (Nankong). Slice four butterflies using the reverse-imaging technique (see page 17). Reassemble and mount butterfly pieces on alternating color as shown; randomly place remaining butterflies. *Pamela Frye*

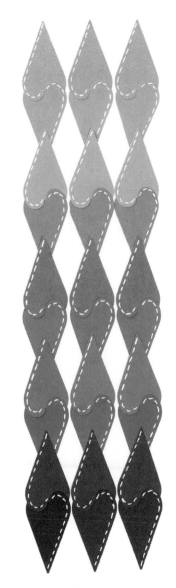

Construct "Windows" of Opportunity

Punched squares can provide "windows" to showcase punched or stamped designs—even small photos. For an 8½ x 11" page, enlarge by 200% and photocopy pattern on page 89; transfer to back of background paper for punch guidelines. Flip 1½" square punch (Family Treasures) over. Insert paper, center guidelines (see Punch positioning, page 16) and punch. Place "windowed" paper over blank background page and lightly trace window squares for art placement guidelines in pencil; remove "windowed" paper. Create designs or crop photos for behind windows; mount elements off-center on placement guidelines for visual interest. Our window designs feature the following punched vellum shapes and stamp: flower leaf (EK Success), small flowers from five-flower corner punch (McGill), silhouette flower and silhouette daisy (both Family Treasures), mini snowflake (Marvy/Uchida) and stamped flower (Judi-Kins). Add strokes of watercolor crayons (Staedtler) and pencils (Sanford, Corp.) for depth. Mount "windowed" paper over designed squares. *Jenna Beegle, Photo Cheryl Rooney*

Interlock an Interesting Border

Interlock punched shapes by linking shapes together to create unique border effects. Punch super jumbo primitive hearts (Emagination Crafts) from gradated shades of paper. Follow the punch progression steps below to interlock (see page 16) shades together as shown beginning at the top of the page with the lightest shade and working down; adhere. Accent with pen stroke stitching (see page 16) in white ink. *Valerie Brincheck*

B&W Neutrals

Isn't it odd that black can be sleekly modern and powerful one moment and elegantly traditional and understated the next? The same goes for white—fresh and crisp one moment, innocently pure and soft the next. When paired together, these "colorless" colors make a strong composition. Without the distraction of color, the unadorned beauty and humble integrity of a black-and-white photo's subject shines through. It's the same with punch art.

Beyond true black and true white, there's a whole spectrum of wonderful black and white shades, softened by hints of many colors—including passive gray and supportive brown—that pair up beautifully with light, neutral tones of cream and ivory. To make up for the lack of color, add a splash of texture with wire, beads, glittery metallics or natural hemp cord for interesting results.

(left) See page 88 for punches and products used.

Weave a Contrasting Border

Floral punch art turns masculine when woven together with eyelet-laden border strips. Slice ½" and ¾" border strips from solid and patterned paper (Creative Impressions). Adhere flowers and petal leaves (both EK Success) layered with mini quasars (Emagination Crafts) and ¼" circles on patterned paper strip. Add eyelets (see page 17) with evenly spaced ⅛" circles punched into strip. Interweave borders at corner; mount onto background with title, journaling blocks and matted photos. *Photos Jennifer Chumbley*

Add Texture to a Lampshade

Transform a plain lampshade—available at craft stores—into a showy accent piece with punch art, eyelets and natural hemp cord. Enlarge and photocopy pattern on page 89 to fit a 6" lampshade or use paper to create a custom-sized pattern—trimming as needed for a perfect fit—for a larger lampshade. Transfer pattern to cardstock. Cut strips of solid and patterned paper (The Robin's Nest, Hot Off The Press) and trim to fit cardstock. Follow the punch progression steps to the right to accent strips with repunched (see page 16) small squares (EK Success, Family Treasures) and to punch 1/16" holes for lacing cord on strips. Add eyelets (see page 17), alternating with ⅛" punched circles to additional strips. Overlap and adhere decorated paper strips to cardstock, alternating patterns as you go; accent with mini triangles. Spread tacky glue (Duncan Enterprises/Aleene's) evenly on back of cardstock; apply to lampshade, using clothespins on upper and lower edges of lampshade to hold cardstock in place until glue dries.

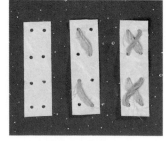

One Punch

Tri Leaf

Leaf cluster punches offer a wide array of design possibilities. You can arrange the leaf clusters in many different ways for an entirely new effect each time. The true allure of punch art is its endless versatility. For example, the color combinations used in the patterns shown below create an organic, earthy feel. With just a little imagination, you can re-create these very same patterns in any other color shown in this book to completely change the overall effect (see page 6). Go on. Give it a try! *Kelly Angard, Michele Gerbrant*

EK Success' tri leaf punch was used to make these classic border patterns. There are countless sizes and shapes of leaf cluster punches that you can experiment with to create your own one-of-a-kind border designs.

Squint your eyes to notice all of the fun shapes going on in the negative space. This intricate-looking pattern starts with a ¾" wide strip of black paper. Slice stems off of monotone-colored leaf clusters; mount in double rows as shown.

For a simple, elegant border, punch leaf clusters from patterned paper (Making Memories). Overlap the top leaf and lower stem of each cluster; mount end-to-end in a straight line as shown.

Dress up single leaf clusters by mounting them alternately, right-side up and upside down, atop a small punched square. Let the stems dangle off of the squares for a contemporary feel.

In this pattern, leaf clusters join together to create a look reminiscent of a European snowflake print. Start with a 1½" wide black paper strip. Adhere ⅛" white paper strips at upper and lower edges of black strip. Slice stems from punched leaf clusters; group into a foursome as shown. Punch ⅛" round dot for center. Repeat to complete border.

Make handsome medallions by assembling four leaf clusters with the top leaves joined in the center. Top each center with a tiny faceted stone to complete.

To create a Caesar-esque border, punch and layer three monochromatic-colored leaf clusters, angled and spaced evenly as shown.

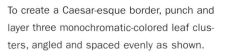

73

Cast Light on an Elizabethan Pattern

Punched shapes take on the illusion of dimension when shaded with watercolor pencils and brushed with a damp paintbrush to mimic the direction of a light source across a pattern—this one similar to a pattern in the *Armada* portrait of Elizabeth I. Begin with a dark background. Punch medium teardrops (Emagination Crafts), small flowers (All Night Media) and 5/16" circles from light-colored cardstock. Adhere punched elements to background in desired pattern, using a ruler to help form straight lines. Add title, nameplate and matted photo. Follow the steps below to "cast light" across the pattern. *Jenna Beegle*

1 *Use a watercolor pencil to draw lines on design to mimic where shadows would fall based on the direction of an imagined or implied light source. Study the art shown to help you get a feel for this concept, or hold an object in front of a sunny window to see how shadows are cast based on an actual light source. Then dampen a paint brush and lightly smudge over pencil, creating a charcoal-like shading effect.*

Reproduce a European Snowflake Design

Six different punched shapes join forces to form intricate yet simple borders inspired by frilly European snowflake designs. Use a dark background. Build white border from top of page down with small diamond (EK Success) repunched with mini quasar (Family Treasures); negative pieces from baroque border punch (All Night Media); small stems, negative pieces from heritage border punch and triple leaves (all Family Treasures); and additional mini quasars. Repeat border in curved fashion for page corner. Add title block and photos; adorn with more punched shapes. Experiment with other intricately shaped punches for your own European snowflake renditions. *Valerie Brincheck, Photos Cynthia Anning*

Punch a Nostalgic Border

Capture a historic vignette with punched photocopies of heritage photos. Flip a 1¼" square (Family Treasures) punch over, center element of each photo that you wish to use and punch (see Punch positioning on page 16). To create mats, punch ten 1⁹⁄₁₆" squares (Family Treasures) from patterned papers (Family Archive, Anna Griffin); repunch with decorative corner rounder (Carl). Stamp (small car and clock, Rubber Stampede; large cars, Classic Status Stamp Co. and Magenta) some of the mats, if desired. Mount photos on mats, tie corners with embroidery floss; mount on page edges to form borders. Add title and journaling blocks. Accent page with photocopied memorabilia, buttons (Buttons Galore) and punched mini diamonds (Family Treasures). *Erikia Ghumm, Photos Pennie Stutzman*

Add Modern Twist to Classic Look

Complement heritage photos with a timeless argyle design with a contemporary twist. Punch 1¼" squares (The Punch Bunch) from patterned paper (MiniGraphics). Mount squares point-to-point on background. Mount a second set of 1¼" squares as shown atop first set. Punch ¾" squares (The Punch Bunch) from solid paper and ⅜" squares (Marvy/Uchida) from patterned paper; layer alternately and mount as shown. Attach eyelets (see page 17) to center of each design. *Alexandra Bleicher*

Dress a "Charm"-ing Window

Create drama with "charm"-ing appeal with charms dangling in punched "windows." Begin by punching 1" squares (Family Treasures), 1½" apart for windows. Punch a ⅛" hole where eyelets will be (see page 17); add eyelets (Impress Rubber Stamps). Open large jump ring with needle-nose pliers (see page 17). Insert one end through eyelet and join with circle on charm (Halcraft); close jump ring. Repeat until windows are filled. Mount 2" wide strip of paper behind windows. *Sarah Fishburn*

Layer Graduated Sizes for Depth

Graduating sizes of layered circles, punched from monochromatic paper colors and accented with black, make this retro-'70s pattern new again. First, center and adhere nine super giant squares (Family Treasures)—in colored paper that complements the cardstock card—to form a patchwork background. Punch several jumbo, large and medium circles (Family Treasures) from papers used for squares. Layer three circles in alternating colors for the square in the center and each of the four corner squares. Layer two circles in alternating colors for the four remaining squares. Adhere all circles and add journaling around punched design. *Michele Gerbrandt*

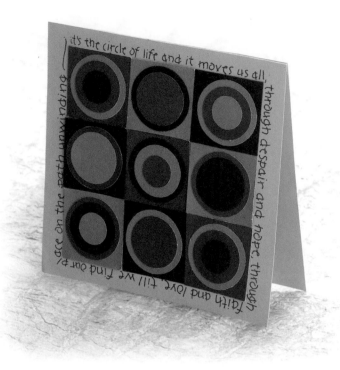

Use Chalk to Mimic Embossing

Lightly chalk around a punched shape to mimic the look of embossed paper. Begin with patterned background (Hot Off The Press). Add gold photo corners (Canson) to photo; mat on cardstock and mount in center of page. Mount matted title and journaling block and gold charm (Creative Beginnings) below photo. Accent page corners and photo edges with jumbo swirls (Nankong), small swirls (EK Success), and large (Emagination Crafts) and small oval (Family Treasures) punches. Follow the steps below to "emboss." *Jenna Beegle, Photo Alexandra Bleicher*

1 To "emboss," hold an extra punched swirl over design and lightly chalk around it with chalk that is one shade darker than background paper.

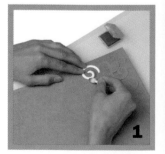

Punch a Folk Art Masterpiece

Traditional folk art creates a perfect backdrop for heritage photos. First, double mat photo with patterned (Anna Griffin) and solid paper; mount in center of page. Use negative pieces from a large vine border punch (Family Treasures) to form a rectangular vine 1" out from photo mat's edge. Accent vine with negative pieces from small vine border punch (Family Treasures), spaced about 1¾" apart for cross vines. Enhance vines with sun layered with small circles and water drops (all EK Success) layered with mini teardrops (Fiskars). Add corner design elements made with splashes (EK Success) layered with mini teardrops over a water drop layered with a mini teardrop. *Jenna Beegle*

Age a Tapestry Border

Repunched shapes, monochromatic colors and chalk create a tapestry border with a weathered look. Start with matted border cut to fit page. Following the punch progression steps shown to the left, punch small teardrop first. Flip large teardrop punch (both Emagination Crafts) over, insert and center punched paper; repunch (see page 16) to form teardrop ring. Assemble teardrop rings with small, positive teardrops, small paw print minus the toes (EK Success) and positive shape that falls from swirl border punch (Family Treasures). Assemble shapes and repeat as needed to cover length of border; trim off any overlap at ends. Lightly chalk (Craf-T Products) punch art for a vintage look. *Alexandra Bleicher*

Piece Together a Patchwork Quilt

Create a charming patchwork quilt border with a collection of patterned papers and geometric shapes, perfect for accenting black-and-white or heritage photos. Begin by punching a number of 1", 1½" and 2" rectangles (Nankong), ½" and 1" squares (Family Treasures), medium triangles (The Punch Bunch), and lower case "I"s (EK Success) out of coordinating solid and patterned papers. Begin the design at one end and arrange shapes in an eye-pleasing manner, leaving at least ⅛" between each punched shape. *Valerie Brincheck*

1 *Use a paintbrush to apply 3-D foiling glue (Duncan Enterprises/Aleene's) to tips of positive and negative suns (Figure 1). Let glue dry until it is semi-clear; glue will still be sticky to the touch.*

2 *Cut eight pieces of crafting foil (Aleene's) from sheet to fit over each punched sun. Apply foil atop dried glue on punched sun, rub gently and carefully peel foil away (Figure 2). Repeat with remaining sets of positive and negative suns.*

Foil Positive and Negative Pieces

Glittery gold foil and tiny glass marbles add sparkly texture to a scrapbook page, while making good use of both the positive and negative punched shapes. For an 8½ x 11" page, freehand cut eight 1¾" squares from cardstock. Flip giant sun (McGill) punch over. Insert squares one at a time, center and punch. You now have eight positive suns and eight negative suns in squares. Follow the steps to the left to apply foil. Mount photo and positive and negative foiled suns on page as shown. To add tiny glass marbles (Halcraft) to negative suns, punch eight ½" circles (Family Treasures) from double-sided adhesive (Therm O Web) and apply marbles (see page 23); remove backing and apply marbled circles to center of suns. Add additional marbles to corners of squares. Finish with hand-drawn title, journaling and fancy pen strokes in gold ink. *Dawn Mabe, Photo Gerri Roberts*

Embellish Stamped Background

For an old-world look, use small punched squares over a stamped background to showcase travel photos. Start with patterned background paper (Scrap Ease) that is stamped randomly in black ink (Tsukineko) with assorted travel-related stamps (Above the Mark, All Night Media, Stampers Anonymous, Stampington & Co.). Adhere small punched black squares (Emagination Crafts) at upper and lower edges in checkerboard fashion, without covering entire background. Add cropped, double-matted photos. String multi-thread yarn (Muench Yarns) in a random, crisscross pattern across each page; secure on back with artists tape. Trace and hand cut title using a lettering template (Cut-It-Up) to finish the spread. *Donna Pittard*

dilemma of paper selection; no paper color is ~~off~~

art itself, the color possibilities are as endless as your imagination!

For the most pleasing rainbow-hued punch art, use only bright papers or only pastel papers; mixing color intensities (see page 13) can drain energy from your design. For rainbow pages, use photos with uncluttered backgrounds or mat photos with solid-colored, black or white cardstock to get a degree of separation between the photo and the background so that your photos won't get lost in the punch art.

(left)
See page 88 for punches and products used.

Punch a Colorful Background

Multidimensional, multicolored rainbow "arcs" are a playful way to put your craft supplies and punches to use. Start by freehand cutting arcs from brightly colored paper; layer and adhere to background in color order shown. Embellish each arc with monochromatic-colored punched shapes, buttons, beads and faceted stones. Create matted title letters using template (Frances Meyer) from patterned marble paper (The Paper Company); adhere above rainbow with self-adhesive foam spacers. Mount parchment-matted photos with foam spacers atop rainbow. Finish with journaling block. *Photos Cheryl Rooney*

Design a Vibrant Gift Bag

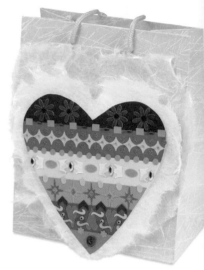

Straighten a rainbow's curves for a loving gift bag accent. Begin with a colored gift bag of choice. Freehand cut cardstock heart with a width 2" less than the bag's width. Freehand cut bold-colored paper strips, layer in order shown and adhere to heart; trim off overlap at heart's edges. Decorate each strip with monochromatic-colored punched shapes, beads, faceted stones and handmade wire swirl (Duncan Enterprises). Adhere heart on heart-shaped layers of torn mulberry paper; mount on gift bag with self-adhesive foam spacers.

Eat Your Punch Art Out!

Take your craft punches to the kitchen to transform ordinary cakes and sweets into extraordinary punch art treats! Begin with baked and cooled cupcakes, frosted with white or tinted frosting. Punch large northern stars, large primitive hearts, small quasars (all Emagination Crafts), large daisies, medium decorative squares and asterisks (all Family Treasures) from edible potato paper; apply color to punched shapes with edible paints and markers (Kidz Baking Klub by Chicago Metallic), following manufacturer's instructions on package. Press shapes into frosting; accent with colored candies and sugar sprinkles. *Idea Becky Laskowski, Bear, Delaware*

Imagine the edible punch art possibilities! See *Memory Makers Punch Your Art Out 1 & 2* for amazing wedding, baby, seasonal, holiday, floral, animal, birthday and specialty themes for your baked goodies.

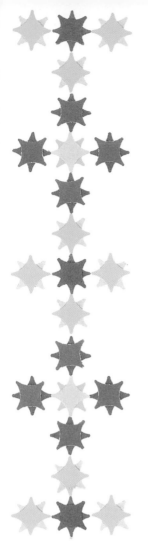

One Punch

Quasar

The small quasar punch is a unique, star-like shape that can make all kinds of funky borders. Incorporate numerous paper colors, tiny glass marbles and more to enhance the designs. Play with the arrangement of the punched quasars for limitless border possibilities.

Kelly Angard, Jenna Beegle

To achieve a serpentine pattern, overlap and layer quasars as shown.

Create a wild, playful border design by layering various-colored quasars in a free-form pattern.

Overlap and assemble punched shapes, vertically and horizontally, to make a simple pattern.

For a bold border statement, lay small black quasars side by side, with points touching. Embellish with mini extension quasars in each center. Note how the use of primary and secondary colors add to this pattern's boldness.

For a retro look, mount a double row of punched quasars, with tips touching as shown, resulting in a circular pattern in the negative space on your background. Add quasars, decorated with tiny glass marbles (Halcraft), in the negative space.

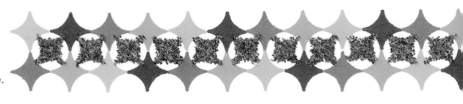

Slice and Reassemble "Sun" Flowers

Walk on the wild side with sliced flowers made with punched and layered suns, reassembled on contrasting-colored strips for visual impact. Mount strips of colored paper on background. Follow the punch progression steps above to slice, reassemble and layer sunflowers using jumbo (Emagination Crafts) and large (McGill) sun punches. Mount different sizes with self-adhesive foam spacers; add sequins for sparkle. *Kelly Angard*

Coordinate Punches With Theme Paper

Some punches and patterned papers seem destined to be together, such as these '60s-style flower punches (widely available; designs vary among manufacturers) that pack a groovy retro punch when used with tie-dyed patterned paper (Hot Off The Press). For frame, embellish patterned paper with punched flowers; curl some of the flowers slightly around a pencil for dimension. For frame or border variations, adhere the positive punched shapes to a white paper strip (top border below) and trim overlap; or trim edges of punched paper strip (lower border) to showcase the negative space left over from punching. Accent flower centers with faceted stones (The Beadery). Try this with snowflake, cloud, star, swirl, tree or heart paper and punch combinations for a "match made in heaven." *Pamela Frye, Photo Ken Trujillo*

Piece Together a Quilt

Patterned papers vary the look of a basic shape when pieced together in a repetitive quilt-like design. Punch large rectangles (Family Treasures) from a variety of light, dark, solid and patterned (FLAX San Francisco) papers; arrange on background starting at upper left corner. Mount first rectangle and work across page in one color, alternating punched shapes ¼" up and ¼" down. Repeat until shapes cover page. Add matted photo to complete design. *Kelly Angard, Photo Denise Richardson*

Punch a Tone-on-Tone Harlequin Pattern

Jewel-toned vellum geometric shapes are paired with monochromatic paper blocks to create a playful yet elegant background. Begin with colored paper over background. Accent blocks as follows: line up small diamond (EK Success) shapes point-to-point in rows; add 1¼" circles (McGill) for perfect polka dot patterns; and mount ⅝" squares (Emagination Crafts) in a simple checkerboard pattern. Adhere matted photos and title block to complete the colorful compilation. *Donna Pittard*

Additional Instructions

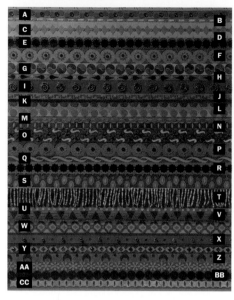

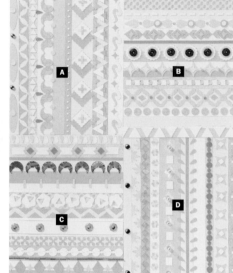

Page 18 **Red**

A–small primitive heart (EC), sequins (Westrim) **B**–zipper border punch (EKS) **C**–diamond (FT), tri dot circles (EKS) **D**–mini diamond extension (FT) **E**–sun (EKS), velvet paper (Wintech) **F**–small quasar (EC), sun (EKS), sequins (Westrim), gold ink (Tsukineko) **G**–splash (EKS), Valerie Brincheck **H**–small teardrop (EC), mini square (EKS) **I**–⅝" circle (FT), wire (Artistic Wire) **J**–chain link (EKS) **K**–bugle beads (Crafts, Etc.) **L**–1⁵⁄₁₆" circle (FT), small quasar (EC), punctuation from upper case alphabet kit (FT) **M**–mini ⅛₆" square (FT), mini thin diamond (FT) **N**–small quasar (EC) **O**–wave border (EKS), punctuation from upper case alphabet kit (FT) **P**–same as "F" above **Q**–swirl border (FT) **R**–same as "D" and "E" above, velvet paper (source unknown) **S**–¹⁄₁₆" circle, mini thin diamond (FT), small oval (FT) **T**–beaded fringe (Hobby Lobby) **U**–⅛" circle **V**–mini triangle (FT), mini rectangle (FT), bugle beads **W**–⅛" circle, mini wide diamond (FT), medium daisy (petals sliced off; FT), Valerie Brincheck **X**–⅛" circle, eyelets (Impress Rubber Stamps) **Y**–small building block (FT), faceted stones **Z**–buttercup (EKS) **AA**–asterisk (ANM) **BB**–sequins **CC**–small quasar (EC), Jenna Beegle

Page 28 **Orange**

A–small building block (FT), mini thin diamond (FT), mini swirl (FT), faceted stones **B**–medium square (Carl), square from patchwork border (EKS), large daisy (FT), faceted stones, Alison Beachem **C**–small scalloped oval (FT), beads (Westrim), ⁵⁄₁₆" circle (FT), mini diamond extension (FT), faceted stones **D**–zipper border (EKS), ½" circle, cone (EKS), eyelets (Impress Rubber Stamps), faceted stones, Alexandra Bleicher **E**–flower power (EKS), mini teardrop extension (FT), ⅛" circle, rectangle (EKS), ³⁄₁₆" circle (EKS), beads (Buttons Galore), decorative cord, Tracy Johnson **F**–folk heart (EKS), diamond (ANM), sequins (Scrappy's Magic Scraps), hexagon (halved; FT), beads, faceted stones

Page 36 **Yellow**

A–wide oval (FT), ¼" circle, deco fasteners (HG/AP), small quasar (halved; EC), tiny triangles (FT), tiny teardrop (FT), splash (EKS), ³⁄₁₆" circle, tiny squares (EKS), medium and large decorative squares (FT), small rectangles (FT), small and tiny triangles (FT), swash (EKS), mini quasar (EC), Alexandra Bleicher **B**–square (FT), tiny rectangle (FT), small primitive heart (EC), small and medium circles (EKS), dot (FT), diamond (FT), small building block (FT), quasar (EC), Valerie Brincheck, Design Lines™ stickers (Mrs. G), large scalloped circle (FT), dingbat from upper case alphabet kit (FT), sequins (Westrim), small and mini quasar (EC), beads (Westrim), small square (FT), ⅛" circle, Alison Beachem, daisy (trimmed; FT), mini diamond (MG), dot (FT), ⁵⁄₁₆" circle (FT), small triangles (FT), Valerie Brincheck **C**–small teardrop (FT), medium rectangle (EKS), medium square (EKS), small square (FT), Design Lines™ sticker (Mrs. G), moon (minus the star; EKS), embossing foil (AMACO), zipper link (EKS), flower (EKS) punched with tiny triangle (FT), diamond (halved lengthwise; EKS), flower eyelets (Stampin FUNaddict), punctuation mark from lower case alphabet kit (FT), ⁵⁄₁₆" circle (EKS), mini thin diamond (FT), bugle beads (Westrim), small diamond (FT), mini quasar (EC) **D**–faceted stones (The Beadery), shining star (halved; EKS), mini square (FT), mini flower (ANM), diamond (EKS), rectangle (EKS), beads (Westrim), small water drop (FT), Design Lines™ sticker (Mrs. G), dot (FT), ¼" circle, small quasar (EC), tiny square (EKS), negative piece from southwest border (FT), negative piece from filmstrip border (MU), Alison Beachem

Key

AMACO=American Art Clay Co.

ANM=All Night Media

EC=Emagination Crafts

EKS=EK Success

FT=Family Treasures

HG/AP=HyGlo/AmericanPin

HOTP=Hot Off The Press

KMA=Keeping Memories Alive

MM=Making Memories

MU=Marvy/Uchida

MG=McGill

Mrs. G=Mrs. Grossman's

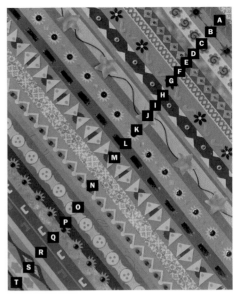

Page 44 Green

A–cross (MG) **B**–pompom (EKS), sequin **C**–dot (EKS) **D**–punctuation from lowercase alphabet kit (FT), small square (EKS) **E**–fleur–de–lis (ANM) **F**–giant birch leaf (FT), faceted stones (Westrim) **G**–small quasar (EC), bead **H**–sun (FT), small moon (ANM) **I**–thin diamond (FT) **J**–small flower (FT), bead **K**–chain link (EKS), small quasar (EC) **L**–small spiral (FT) **M**–patterned paper (DMD Industries), large sunburst (Carl), circle (FT), prism paper (Grafix) **N**–medium circle (FT), small diamond (ANM), thin diamond (FT), small circle (EKS), Design Lines™ sticker (Mrs. G) **O**–medium moon (EKS), small circle (EKS), bead, Erikia Ghumm **P**–small square (EKS), rectangle (EKS), embossing foil (AMACO) **Q**–snidely corner punch (EC), Jenna Beegle **R**–Design Lines™ sticker (Mrs. G), dot (FT), buttons (Buttons Galore), Erikia Ghumm **S**–large northern star (EC), sequin (Westrim) **T**–mini rectangle (EKS) **U**–small building block (FT) **V**–patterned paper (KMA), jumbo water splat (EC), sequin (Westrim) **W**–small flower (FT), dot (FT) **X**–small quasar (EC), mini quasar (EC), Design Lines™ sticker (Mrs. G), bead (Westrim), Alison Beachem **Y**–small drop (FT), Jenna Beegle **Z**–scalloped square (FT), deco fastener (HG/AP), Alexandra Bleicher **AA**–small circle (FT) **BB**–large oval (FT) **CC**–gigantic daisy (FT), faceted stone (Westrim) **DD**–pompom (EKS), wire (Artistic Wire), bead (Westrim), Joan Gosling **EE**–square (FT), mini quasar (EC), beads, Michele Gerbrandt **FF**–large oval (FT), moon (EKS), small quasar (EC), small circle (EKS), sequins **GG**–medium oval (FT), embossing foil (AMACO), Design Lines™ sticker (Mrs. G) **HH**–small circle (EKS) **II**–patterned paper (Paper Adventures), large heart (EC), bead (Westrim) **JJ**–gigantic swirl (FT), sequins **KK**–swirl (EKS), dot (FT) **LL**–thin diamond (FT) **MM**–triangle (FT), small square (FT), dot (FT) **NN**–small circle (EKS) **OO**–mini, small and medium squares (FT), Amanda Wilson **PP**–tear drop (EC), faceted stones **QQ**–patterned paper (HOTP), jumbo star (Carl), buttons (Buttons Galore) **RR**–mini fleur–de–lis (ANM), small square (Fiskar) **SS**–mini teardrop (MG) **TT**–patterned paper (KMA), flower power (EKS), bead (Westrim) **UU**–water drop (EKS), sequins **VV**–small sun (quartered; Carl), mini circle (FT) **WW**–mini squares (EKS) **XX**–small daisy (petals sliced off; EKS) **YY**–holly leaf (EKS), rectangle (EKS) **ZZ**–mini sun (ANM)

Page 52 Blue

A–mini ¼" circle (FT), moon sticker (Mrs. G), embossing foil (AMACO) **B**–extra large and large decorative square (FT), shining star (EKS), quasar extension (FC), Valerie Brincheck **C**–small teardrop (EC), medium and mini square (FT), diamond (ANM), bead (Westrim), Pamela Frye **D**–large square (FT), pompom (EKS), mini ¼" circle (FT), ⅛" circle extension (EC), bead (Westrim), Pamela Frye **E**–patterned paper (HOTP), large daisy (FT), small ⅜" square (FT), medium swirl (FT), Pamela Frye **F**–extra large decorative square (FT), asterisk (FT alphabet kit), flower (EKS), faceted stone (Westrim), Pamela Frye **G**–patterned paper (Colors by Design), large flower (FT), small building block (FT), mini flower (FT), mini ⅛" square (FT), bead (Westrim), Pamela Frye **H**–extra large decorative square (FT), sprinkles (EKS), wave border (EKS), bead (Westrim), Valerie Brinckeck

Page 62 Purple

A–medium building block (FT) **B**–northern star (EC), sequin (Westrim) **C**–patterned paper (Impress Rubber Stamps), geometric shape from uppercase alphabet kit (FT), small swirl (FT) **D**–patterned paper (HOTP) **E**–small square (FT), mini diamond extension (FT), bead (Westrim), Michele Gerbrandt **F**–"X" from lowercase alphabet kit (FT), Pamela Frye **G**–embossing foil (AMACO), daisy (EKS), dot extension (EC), wave border (EKS), Pamela Frye **H**–diamond (EKS), eyelet (A.W. Cute Stickers 'n' Stuff), Design Lines™ sticker (Mrs. G), Pamela Frye **I**–patterned paper (FLAX San Francisco) **J**–giant star (Carl), wire (Artistic Wire), Beth Rogers **K**–medium sun (Carl), mini square extension (FT), sequins (Westrim), Pamela Frye **L**–rectangle (MG), raffia (Paper Adventures) **M**–square (FT), sun (FT), dot extension (FT), Pamela Frye **N**–snidely corner punch (EC), beads (Westrim), Jenna Beegle **O**–circle (EKS), triple dot (EKS), medium circle (FT), medium diamond (FT), Valerie Brincheck **P**–patterned paper (source unknown), medium sun (Carl), small quasar (EC), faceted stone (The Beadery) **Q**–chain link border (EKS), Design Lines™ sticker (Mrs. G) **R**–small and large teardrops (EC), beads (Westrim) **S**–holly leaf (EKS), beads **T**–pinwheel (EKS)

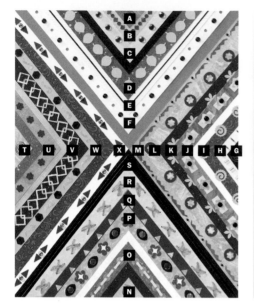

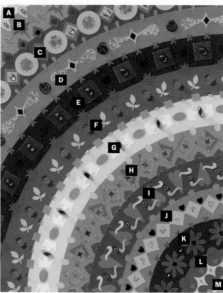

Page 70 **B&W/Neutrals**

A–wire (Artistic Wire) **B**–¼" circle (FT), patterned paper (MM), small square (EKS) **C**–faceted stones **D**–patterned paper (HOTP), stem leaf (EKS), Kathleen Aho **E**–patterned paper (The Crafter's Workshop), Design Lines™ sticker (Mrs. G) **F**–dot (FT), ¼" circle (FT) **G**–wire (Artistic Wire) **H**–beads **I**–patterned paper (MM), small sun (EKS), small spiral (EC) **J**–patterned paper (Rocky Mountain Scrapbook Co.), rectangle (FT), square (EKS), faceted stones (The Beadery) **K**–patterned paper (The Robin's Nest), daisy (EKS) **L**–patterned paper (The Robin's Nest), circle (EKS), mini flower (ANM), Jenna Beegle **M**–zig zag corner punch (ANM), beads (Scrappy's Magic Scraps) **N**–patterned paper (source unknown), wire (Artistic Wire) **O**–⅛" circle (FT), rectangle (EKS) **P**–patterned paper (MM), medium flower (EKS), oval (EKS), small quasar (EC), ⅛" circle (FT), Sylvie Abecassis **Q**–small triangle (FT) **R**–dot (FT) **S**–Design Lines™ sticker (Mrs. G) **T**–wire (Artistic Wire) **U**–mini flower (EKS) **V**–square (EKS & FT), Pamela Frye **W**–swirl (EKS), sequins (MS) **X**–cone (EKS), beads (Scrappy's Magic Scraps)

Page 80 **Rainbow**

A–moon (EKS), mini ¼" circle (FT) **B**–water drop (EKS), northern star (EC), small diamond (ANM), large diamond (FT), sequins **C**–large 1¼" circle (FT), medium ⅝" square (FT), square (EKS), sun (EKS), embossing foil (AMACO), small tear drop (FT), faceted stones, Alexandra Bleicher **D**–large tear drop (EC), small quasar (EC), mini wide diamond (FT), "X" from lowercase alphabet kit (FT), wire (Artistic Wire) **E**–extra large decorative square (FT), patterned paper (A.W. Cute Stickers 'n' Stuff), small ½" circle (FT), shining star (EKS), buttons (Buttons Galore) **F**–leaf (FT), mini flower (FT), patterned paper (FLAX San Francisco), small rectangle (EKS), beads, Jenna Beegle **G**–crown (ANM), medium oval (FT), beads **H**–dudley corner punch (EC), mini diamond extension (FT), medium building block (FT), mini dot extension (FT), small scalloped oval (FT), Alison Beachem **I**–primitive heart (EC), wave border (EKS), small flower (FT), beads (Westrim) **J**–extra large decorative square (FT), mini ⅛" square (FT), mini triangle (FT), heart sequins **K**–large daisy (FT), square from patchwork border (EKS), small scalloped oval (FT), faceted stones **L**–quasar (EC), mini ¼" circle (FT), mini ⅛" circle (FT), beads (Westrim) **M**–asterisk from lowercase alphabet kit (FT)

Page 3
Romanesque Wreath

Embellish a lush border design of leaves with pen strokes, beads and foam spacers to create an elegant and dramatic photo frame or border. Begin by drawing a circle to fit page or use a circle-cropped photo for a guide; adhere mega twigs (Nankong) punched from velvet paper (Wintech) end to end around circle. Punch a second set of leaves in lighter monochromatic color and add pen strokes and ink highlights to leaves. Trim leaves off stem; adhere cut leaves in circle atop darker leaves using self-adhesive foam spacers. Thread beads and wrap around design, giving the illusion beads are "woven" around the wreath. *Michele Gerbrandt*

Page 6
To make border, overlap the top leaf and lower stem of each tri leaf (EK Success), mount end-to-end in a straight line as shown. *Michele Gerbrandt*

Patterns

Use these helpful patterns to complete specific scrapbook pages and projects featured in this book. Simply enlarge and photocopy the patterns as needed to fit your scrapbook page or project size.

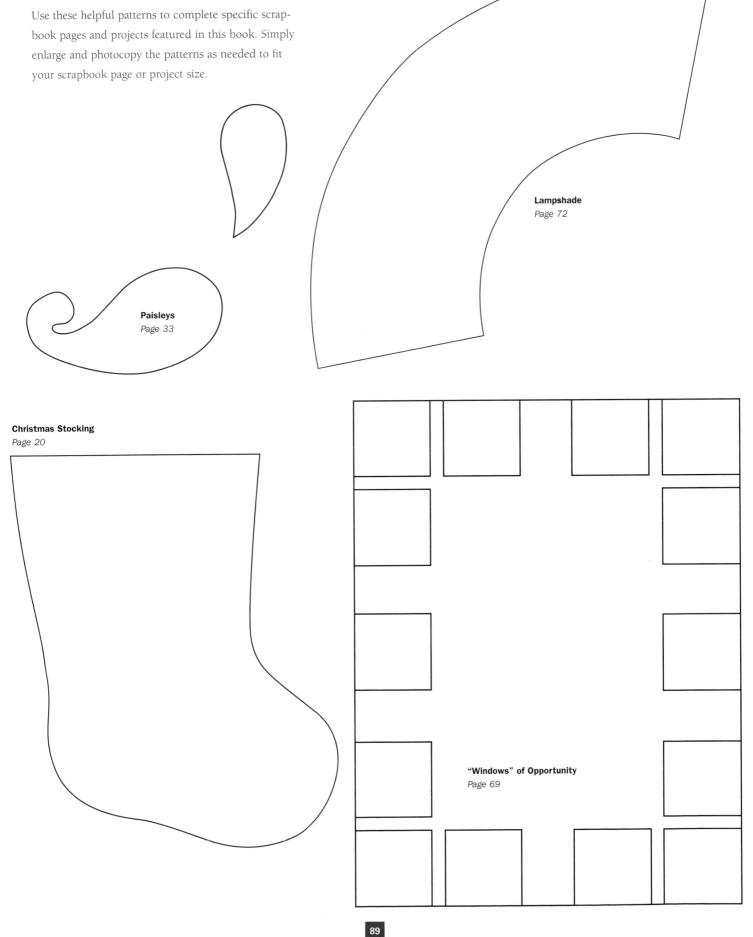

Lampshade
Page 72

Paisleys
Page 33

Christmas Stocking
Page 20

"Windows" of Opportunity
Page 69

Sources

Thanks to the following companies that manufacture products used to create the art featured in this book. Please check your local retailers to find these products. In addition, we have made every attempt to properly credit the trademarks and brand names of the items mentioned in this book. We apologize to any companies that have been listed incorrectly, and we would appreciate hearing from you.

Above the Mark
530-666-6648

All My Memories
888-553-1998

All Night Media®, Inc./Plaid
Enterprises
Wholesale Only
800-782-6733

American Art Clay Co./AMACO
800-374-1600

Anna Griffin, Inc.
888-817-8170

Art Institute Glitter
877-909-0805

Artistic Wire Ltd.™
630-530-7567

A.W. Cute Stickers 'n' Stuff
877-560-6943

The Beadery®/Greene Plastics
Corporation
401-539-2432

Buttons Galore
856-753-0165

Canson, Inc.®
Wholesale Only
800-628-9283

Carl Mfg. USA, Inc.
800-257-4771

Chicago Metallic/A Division of C.M.
Products Inc.
847-438-2171

Classic Status Stamp Co.
231-547-9784

Clearsnap Inc.
800-448-4862

C.M. Offray & Son
800-344-5533

Colorbök Wholesale Only
800-366-4660

Colors by Design
800-832-8436

Craf-T Products
Wholesale Only
507-235-3996

Crafter's Pride
800-277-6850

The Crafter's Workshop
877-CRAFTER or 877-272-3837

Crafts, Etc. Ltd.
800-888-0321

Creative Beginnings/The Bead
Shoppe®
800-367-1739

Creative Imaginations
800-942-6487

The C-Thru® Ruler Company
800-243-8419

Cut-It-Up™
530-389-2233

Design Originals
800-877-7820

D.J. Inkers™
800-325-4890

DMC Corp.
www.dmc.usa.com

DMD Industries, Inc.
800-805-9890

Duncan Enterprises
559-291-4444

EK Success™
800-524-1349

Emagination Crafts Inc.
630-833-9521

The Family Archives™
888-622-6556

Family Treasures, Inc.®
800-413-2645

Fiskars, Inc.
800-950-0203

Frances Meyer, Inc.®
800-372-6237

Grafix®
800-447-2349

Halcraft USA, Inc.
Wholesale Only
212-376-1580

Hobby Lobby
800-888-0321

Hot Off The Press
800-227-9595

HyGlo®/AmericanPin
480-968-6475

Image Matters™
800-849-3390

Impress Rubber Stamps
206-901-9101

Judi-Kins
310-515-1115

Keeping Memories Alive™
800-419-4949

Kolo™
888-828-0367

Lasting Impressions for Paper, Inc.
800-9-EMBOSS or (800) 936-2677

Magenta Rubber Stamps
800-565-5254

Making Memories
800-286-5263

Martha Stewart Living
800-950-7130

Marvy®Uchida
800-541-5877

McGill Inc.
800-982-9884

MiniGraphics, Inc.
Wholesale Only
800-442-7035

Mrs. Grossman's Paper Co.
800-429-4549

Muench Yarns
451-883-6375

Nag Posh™
800-333-3279

Nankong Enterprises, Inc.
Wholesale Only
302-731-2995

The Paper Catalog (FLAX San
Francisco)
888-727-3763

The Paper Company™
800-426-8989

Paper Adventures®
800-727-0699

Pergamano
www.pergamano.com

Provo Craft®
888-577-3545

The Punch Bunch
Wholesale Only
254-791-4209

Ranger Industries, Inc.
800-244-2211

The Robin's Nest Press
435-789-5387

Rocky Mountain Scrapbook Co.
801-785-9695

Rubber Stampede
800-423-4135

Rubber Stamps of America
800-553-5031

Sanford Corp.
800-323-0749

The Scrapbook Wizard™
Wholesale Only
801-947-0019

Scrap Ease®
800-642-6762

Scrappy's Magic Scraps
972-385-1838

Sonburn, Inc./A Division of Mafcote
Industries
800-527-7505

Staedtler®, Inc.
800-927-7723

Stamp Studio, Inc.
208-288-0300

Stampers Anonymous/The Creative
Block
440-333-7941

Stampin FUNaddict
208-465-0500

Stampington & Company
877-STAMPER or 877-782-6737

Starry Night Creations™
763-420-2411

Therm O Web, Inc.
800-323-0799

3M Stationery
800-364-3577

Tsukineko®, Inc.
800-769-6633

Westrim Crafts/Memories Forever®
800-727-2727

Wintech International Corp.
800-263-6043

Artist Index

Bibliography

Mella, Dorothee L. *The Language of Color*. New York: Warner Books, Inc., 1988.

Westgate, Alice. *The Complete Color Directory*. New York: Watson-Guptill Publications, 1999.

Punch Index

The punch shapes shown here and on pages 93, 94 and 95 are some of the ones used most frequently throughout this book and are shown for your reference. Not all punches used in projects are shown. Punch shapes are shown at 100% but may vary by manufacturer.

Jumbo Punches

PRIMITIVE HEART

HEART

CLOUD

CIRCLE

SQUARE

TWIG

OAK LEAF

FERN

SUN

BUTTERFLY

FLOWER

Large Punches

CHEVRON/BUILDING
BLOCK

CIRCLE

CIRCLE

SQUARE

SUN

DAISY

SWIRL/SPIRAL

BIRCH LEAF

HEART

SHELL

FLOWER
SILHOUETTE

FLEUR-DE-LIS

IVY LEAF

WHITE OAK LEAF

GRAPEVINE LEAF

OAK LEAF

FLOWER POT

ASH LEAF

DRAGONFLY

HAWTHORN LEAF

Punch Index continued

Mini & Extended Reach Punches

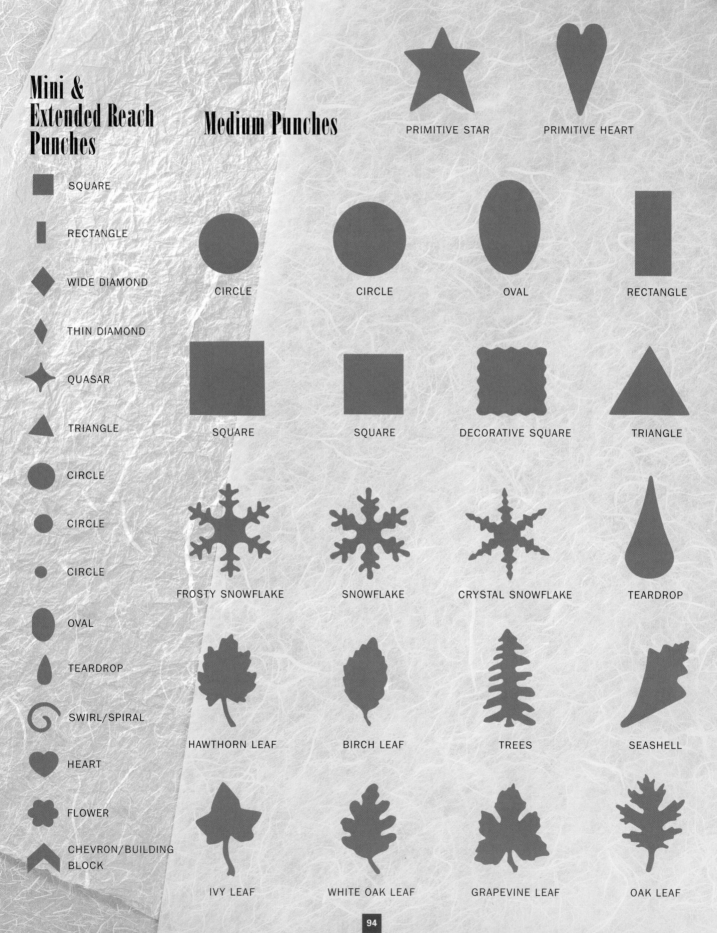

- ■ SQUARE
- ▪ RECTANGLE
- ◆ WIDE DIAMOND
- ◆ THIN DIAMOND
- ✦ QUASAR
- ▲ TRIANGLE
- ● CIRCLE
- ● CIRCLE
- ● CIRCLE
- ● OVAL
- TEARDROP
- SWIRL/SPIRAL
- ♥ HEART
- FLOWER
- CHEVRON/BUILDING BLOCK

Medium Punches

PRIMITIVE STAR

PRIMITIVE HEART

CIRCLE

CIRCLE

OVAL

RECTANGLE

SQUARE

SQUARE

DECORATIVE SQUARE

TRIANGLE

FROSTY SNOWFLAKE

SNOWFLAKE

CRYSTAL SNOWFLAKE

TEARDROP

HAWTHORN LEAF

BIRCH LEAF

TREES

SEASHELL

IVY LEAF

WHITE OAK LEAF

GRAPEVINE LEAF

OAK LEAF

Small Punches

CHAIN LINK	 BUTTERFLY	CHEVRON/BUILDING BLOCK	BIRCH LEAF
CIRCLE	CIRCLE	CROWN	TRI LEAF
DIAMOND	DRAGONFLY	FLEUR-DE-LIS	LEAF #1
GARDEN FLOWER	FLOWER	FLOWER	OAK LEAF
FLOWER POWER	LOTUS	POMPOM	BUTTERCUP
PETAL LEAF	FOLK HEART	ICE CREAM CONE	OVAL
SPLASH	QUASAR	RECTANGLE	DECORATIVE SQUARE
SNOWFLAKE	SWIRL/SPIRAL	SQUARE	LEAF #2
STAR	FOLK STAR	SHINING STAR	SUN
WAVE	WATER DROP	TEARDROP	TRIANGLE

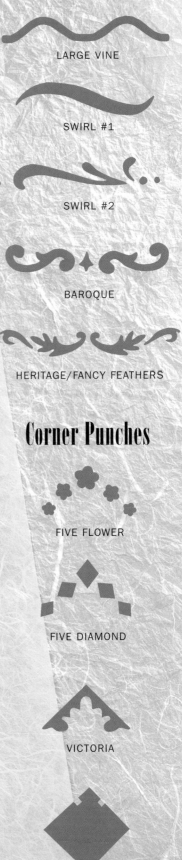

Border Punches

LARGE VINE

SWIRL #1

SWIRL #2

BAROQUE

HERITAGE/FANCY FEATHERS

Corner Punches

FIVE FLOWER

FIVE DIAMOND

VICTORIA

DECORATIVE CORNER

Index